STOP

FIGHTING

TO GET ALONG

Practical, Painless Ways to

Improve Communication, Interactions

& Conflict Resolution Skills in Marriage

Debra Macleod, B.A., J.D.

Paperback edition: ISBN 978-1-990640-10-0
Ebook edition: ISBN 978-1-990640-11-7

Cover design by Caroline Léger

MarriageSOS.com

TABLE OF CONTENTS

INTRODUCTION

Is This Book For You? Checking Off the Boxes

Does your marriage ever feel like a battle zone? Maybe there are open hostilities or maybe it's more of a cold war situation. Regardless, I suspect you've had enough of acting and feeling like enemies. Good. Because this book, *Stop Fighting to Get Along*, can do more than just call a truce between you and your spouse: it can transform you from bitter enemies to the sweetest of allies.

In my capacity as a couples' mediator, I've worked with countless couples who just couldn't seem to get along. In fact, I used to have an intake form in my office that included a list of issues for new clients to check off if applicable. To help me gain some insight into the overall habits and dynamics of the couple's relationship, the first part of the form included issues like always **arguing**, **walking on eggshells**, a **lack of warmth or affection**, chronic **negativity**, and an **inability to communicate** without it turning into a big fight or days of **the silent treatment**, et cetera.

In the second part, I was looking to get my head around what each person's complaints were about their spouse. So, among other things, the list included things like they're always **angry**, **micromanaging** or **nagging**, they're **defensive**, they have a **short fuse**, **stubborn**, **cold**, they pass **blame**, they're too **critical** or **sarcastic**, they're **selfish** or always on their phone or computer. It also included things like, **I feel unloved**, **unheard**, **misunderstood**, **disrespected**, **not prioritized** and—this was always a big one—**unappreciated** by my spouse.

Finally, the third part of this form asked about specific areas of conflict in the marriage. The options here were things like **money**, **sex** and intimacy, **parenting**, **housework**, in-laws, **divided loyalties**, socializing, the **use of technology** and so on.

Again, the idea was for clients to check off just a few of these items—yet instead of checking off the two or three that applied to them, many clients returned the form with a scribbled note saying they'd checked off the two or three that *didn't* apply to them! It's funny in a sad sort of way, isn't it?

But I'll bet that's how you feel sometimes. That you and your partner can't communicate without blowing up or shutting down, and there is a constant strain on your relationship. You may feel that you can't enjoy each other's company in an easygoing way, or work through your problems in a mature way, one that strengthens your marriage instead of chips away at it.

You might be struggling with unflattering personality traits and behaviors that are making it hard to live with your spouse—or that are making it hard for your spouse to live with you. If those are the kinds of boxes you're checking off, then this book is probably for you—and by you, I mean one or both of you.

The great thing about a book like this is that it allows an individual spouse to take the initiative and prompt a change in the marriage dynamics in a positive, low-conflict way. That's important, since if you're already fighting to get along, or if your spouse is showing challenging behavior, then it probably is just you at this point. That's okay. **You have more power than you think to effect a change on your own.** And maybe once things are more peaceful, your spouse will be willing to flip through these pages themselves and do a little self-reflection. So regardless of whether you're reading alone or you're both doing this together, you're covered.

My Approach and The Evolution of This Book

After law school, I began to work in divorce mediation. It was then that I realized how many couples were divorcing even after trying counseling. I had many clients tell me the same thing: the time they spent with their spouse in my office was the most effectively they had communicated in a long time.

That made me think that an alternative to counseling would be useful. Accordingly, I changed the nature of my practice from divorce mediation to couples' / marital mediation designed to help people **save their marriage and stay together.** I called my practice, suitably enough, Marriage SOS.

In practice and in all of my material, I encourage spouses to be fair in terms of understanding and respecting each other's needs, perspectives and feelings: I also encourage them to be aware of how each of them is contributing to the conflict, which includes being able to identify and manage their own and their partner's challenging personality traits and behavior, including possible manipulations— because people are people, and self-determination is essential.

Striking that balance is the basis of my **"Fair, but Aware"** approach, which stems from my background. After all, legal and mediation training variously teach a person to be fair but aware, and to consider things from multiple angles.

One of the great things about a mediation-based approach is that, although contextual, it is generally a partnership-focused process that tries to maintain or improve the overall relationship while at the same time respecting and empowering both people in it. It doesn't diagnose people or take sides, it doesn't endure finger-pointing or excessive self-focus, it doesn't dwell on the past or the negative, and it doesn't try to solve a couple's problems for them. Rather, it helps them understand and resolve their own problems while learning how to avoid future ones. That's why many people prefer it for relationship help, and why I drew inspiration from it, and various conflict resolution principles, regardless of whether I was working with both spouses or just one of them.

Yet there has to be more to it when working with couples. Such work requires a certain level of **innovation and softness** that goes beyond resolving conflict or improving day to day interactions to actually **enhance overall feelings of love, devotion and intimacy** in the marriage. You'll find that goal in every insight and strategy, even if it doesn't always seem like it.

To that end, I've always believed that people who work with struggling couples or spouses should not just have professional experience with marriage, but personal experience, too.

At the time of writing this book, my husband Don and I have been married for over twenty years, and writing and collaborating for as long. That means I'm no stranger to married and family life, and there's hardly a page in this book where I haven't drawn upon that experience—both of our experiences, really—to make the content as relevant and usable as possible.

So that's my approach. Yet as with any approach, it isn't the only one out there and it isn't right for all people or all situations. There are many resources and options available to you, from mental health professionals to lawyers, depending on your preferences, specific circumstances or needs, or how those might change.

One thing I will say, though—no matter how many people call themselves marriage experts, I believe that you are the true expert in your relationship. It is my opinion that people who are otherwise happy and functional are able to improve their own situations once they have some fresh insights and ideas to draw from. And I intend to give you some of those **as quickly as possible!** The only thing worse than languishing in a miserable marriage is languishing in a miserable marriage for one day more than you have to. I have always hated the idea of a practitioner doling out information on a weekly or monthly basis. People need help faster than that. If they don't get it, they lose motivation and even hope.

That's why I've made the material herein as accessible and—believe it or not—enjoyable as possible under the circumstances, and you may be surprised to find it is a much easier and more pleasant read than you might expect from a book like this. Who knows, maybe you'll want to read the whole thing in a day or two. That's because, when you're making progress, it feels good and you want to keep going. And I want you to feel good about yourself, your spouse, and your marriage.

How This Book Works

The truth is, communication isn't always about talking and it certainly isn't about pointing fingers and complaining about each other. Rather, it's about making an **emotional, mental and physical connection**. It's about exchanging information, ideas or feelings which in turn leads to an understanding and a feeling of closeness and happy solidarity.

Talking isn't the only way to achieve this state of being. It's one way. There are times when it works great, and times when it doesn't work at all. I have had clients who were brilliant communicators at work and who were masters when it came to using words—lawyers, publicists, artists and writers—but yet they were fighting to get along with their own spouse. These were people who speak on the world's stage yet when it came to their marriage, they'd say to me, "We just can't talk to each other."

That's because it isn't just about words and how good we are at using them. Rather, it's about our relationship and the vibes, habits and dynamics within it. It's about **how our personality, emotions, thoughts, behaviors and so on intersect with those of our spouse**, and how well we **understand** our spouse, ourselves and the situation. It's about how well we **collaborate** and work as a team to solve our problems in a positive and lasting way, how **motivated** we are to do that, and how **connected** we feel.

Accordingly, I'm going to give you an inventory of focused, creative ways to take back your marriage, your happiness and your sanity. And I'm going to do that in three parts.

Part one will focus on the interactions between you, and the dynamics in your marriage. This is essentially how you treat each other, your various habits in the marriage, and how your personality traits and behaviors are playing off each other.

From finger-pointing and defensiveness to divided loyalties and short fuses, and everything in between, every relationship has its own vibe and its own set of habits. The good news is, there's a lot you can do right now, even on your own, to start improving the vibe and breaking those habits. From technology to intimacy, the dynamics in your marriage need to improve as soon as possible.

This is important content, all delivered in a straightforward way. There's no tiptoeing around issues or behaviors here, there's no avoiding responsibility for your own part in your marriage problems. If you want to save your marriage, you want to know this.

In part two, I'll help you and your partner get to the point where you can have a fabulous conversation about anything, including problems you have or that come up in the marriage. You're going to learn how to decode your spouse—and that's going to make all the difference in your marriage. It shouldn't be frustrating or hard to talk to each other and it doesn't have to be.

In addition to learning how to understand each other better, you'll also learn how to manage those more destructive communication habits: defensiveness, blaming each other, the silent treatment, those pointless fact-based arguments and emotional onslaughts of anger or tears. This stuff is tough to deal with. Don't be hard on yourself if you're struggling with these things.

Instead, be proud that you're taking the initiative to improve matters and remove these communication landmines from your marriage. Frankly, there are too many people who complain about their marriages and partners for years—decades, even!—but never take any steps to make a change.

In part three, I'll help you turn the entire ship around—no more arguing about every little thing, no more assuming the worst about each other, no more fighting and hard feelings and walking on eggshells, and so on. We'll head to calmer waters.

And in the middle of those calm waters, you'll find an island of common ground. Here, you'll rebuild your marriage on the foundation of a romantic friendship. Enough of the adversarial nonsense. You should be each other's greatest advocates in life, and I'll do my best to help you get there.

Yet despite my and your best efforts, some people are tough nuts to crack. That's why we'll talk about how to manage more difficult partners, whether they throw adult temper tantrums or just constantly let you down.

Moving on, I'll show you how to resolve those specific and stubborn areas of conflict in your marriage. There's no point talking about your problems if you don't take practical steps to move past them. Yet too many couples dread this part. After all, it takes a little work.

But here's the thing—couples who do manage to move past their problems in a practical way end up feeling incredibly confident and proud of their marriages. It creates a strong sense of accomplishment and solidarity. **This is how couples use conflict to strengthen their relationship instead of weakening it. Yes, it can be done.**

When it comes to the way all of this content is presented in this book, there is a method to the madness. I've laid everything out in three general parts—interactions, communication and conflict resolution—because it helps to bring structure to what we're doing here.

But I've also done this because the content you'll find within has a cumulative effect. It works like this. Once you improve your interactions (the way you treat each other), much of your communication (the way you talk to each other) naturally improves.

And once you improve both your interactions and your communication, you'll find that some of the conflicts in your relationship (the things you argue about) go away on their own. No, not all of it, by any means, but certainly enough that it warrants taking this approach.

As for those stubborn conflicts that do remain—whether they're about your finances, your priorities, your sex life, your phones, your lifestyle choices or habits—you'll find they are easier to manage, since your relationship has already improved in some important ways. You're therefore in a much better position to tackle those specific areas of conflict.

But perhaps the biggest benefit of this book's three-part structure is that it provides a holistic, overarching "big picture" view of how to understand and improve marital communication, interactions and conflict. That's why I advise people to read all three parts, in their entirety and in order. You never know when something will resonate with you or become relevant. It's always better to know a little too much than not quite enough.

Another advantage of this read-everything-in-order approach is that it forces you to be less impulsive or reactionary, and to think about your situation objectively, comprehensively, and from multiple angles, before you decide which insights or strategies are relevant to your relationship, and whether and how to incorporate them into your marriage.

No matter what happens or what you choose to do, you do not want to look back with regret upon something you said or did, or didn't say or do. Nothing is worse than that kind of regret. Nobody wants to have second thoughts when it comes to something as important as marriage.

So by all means, binge-read the book, but put real thought into how you're going to use its content. Make the most of this important endeavor and get it right the first time!

Put In the Work

To help you do that, I've included a number of questions at the end of each part of this book. These are designed to help you work through the material in a practical way.

I highly recommend that you have a pen and scribbler nearby and take the time to do this. Putting pen to paper like this can be extremely useful and enlightening. Questions can be catalysts, and even a question that doesn't seem that profound on the surface can take you to a deeper place.

So put in the work—although to be honest, it won't seem like work. It will seem like you are liberating yourself, your spouse, and your marriage from the constraints of miscommunication, misunderstanding and miserableness. And the sooner you can do that, the sooner you and your spouse can show the world that you're lovers and not fighters.

PART ONE:

How to Get Along Better: Improving Spousal Interactions ASAP

And They Lived Happily @#%&! Ever After

When people talk about what makes them happy in life, when they talk about what makes them feel fulfilled and what gives them feelings of love and satisfaction, a successful, long-term marriage is at the top of the list. There is simply no substitute for a *happy* marriage. It is one of the most reliable paths to find meaning, companionship and joy in life, and it provides the safest, most secure environment in which to raise children who have a sense of belonging and well-being. It's the ideal we all strive for.

And they lived happily ever after....

But just how in the hell did they manage to do that, you might wonder, your thoughts fuming as you reflect upon how selfish, unappreciative, or defensive your spouse is, or why they don't take your complaints seriously, or why they spend too much money on junk and too little time at home. You begin to think about how things have cooled off in the bedroom while every conversation only seems to get more heated.

While I can't guarantee you a happy ending, I can tell you for certain that many spouses have been exactly where you are—in the midst of anger, pain, resentment, confusion, hopelessness, profound worry—and I have helped them work their way through that to emerge with a marriage that was more mature, loving, committed, easygoing and fun than ever...a marriage where they felt heard and adored above all others, and where they made their spouse feel that way, too.

Every marriage has weaknesses and strengths, ups and downs, terrible habits and glimmers of light. Every happy marriage has a history. You know when you're walking along the beach and you see that elderly couple holding hands and you think, "Wow, they made it"? They did. But what you don't see as you watch them saunter lovingly through the warm sand is what they've gone through to get to that beach.

You don't see the hurtful things they've said or done to each other over the years. You don't see the struggles they've had or the mistakes they've made. You don't see the thousand times they've argued and made up, or the many times that one of them was ready to give up but the other held on and said, "Wait," and they did, and the love returned. You don't see how they were imperfect, and out of that, managed to create a life that was perfect in its own way.

Even if it doesn't feel that way right now, this is a love story. Your love story. And with some patience, humility, work and little luck, that happy ending and stroll along the beach might just be yours. Too optimistic? Maybe. Or maybe a little optimism is exactly what you need to get this endeavor off to a good start. Just remember that we're not going for a fairy tale ending, here. We're going for something much better than that—a happy marriage, right here in the real world.

Here in part one, the focus is on the way you and your spouse interact with each other. You might assume that means we're going to launch straight into an analysis of that, or that I'm going to start using unnecessarily complicated jargon to explain unnecessarily complicated concepts. We're not, and I'm not.

Instead, we're going to keep things sensible and straightforward. We're also going to start at the real beginning—and that's with you. And if that isn't something you want to do or feel is necessary to do, then perhaps that's all the more reason to do it. Regardless, as you'll eventually see, I have my reasons for starting here, and they are reasons that will ultimately work in your best interests. Be patient. Don't rush the process. We'll get everywhere we need to go.

The Marriage Machine

We live in a world where people are very good at pointing out another person's flaws, but not so good at acknowledging their own. This is even more evident when it comes to marriage.

When we're frustrated and emotional, when we're angry or resentful, when we feel unloved or unappreciated or unheard by our spouse, it's all too easy to start pointing fingers. It's all too easy to feel wounded and mistreated, and this can make us lose sight of how we are contributing to the habits and dynamics in the marriage. We're too focused on how our spouse is hurting us or disrespecting us, and how we need them to change.

And guess what? At the same time that we're thinking and feeling this way, our spouse is also thinking and feeling this way. No wonder it's so hard to make a change.

And yet if things are to change, each person does need to get the point where they are willing to reflect upon their own behavior and commit to changing it. Because as life has no doubt already shown you, you cannot change or control another person. That includes your spouse. You can only change and control yourself.

Some people panic when they hear this. They think that unilateral change isn't powerful enough. They're looking for a secret formula, magic spell or expert tip that will make their partner fall into line. Those things don't exist. They don't have to.

Why? Because of the handy little fact that every action has a reaction. Every action you perform (or don't perform, as the case may be) in your marriage, every attitude and vibe you put (or don't put) out there, directly influences how your spouse will react to you.

Every stimulus evokes a response. You press on the gas pedal, and the car goes fast. You take your foot off the gas pedal, and the car slows down. You pour sand in the gas tank, and the car breaks down. To show you that this is as true for marriage as it is for machines, let's see it in action.

I was working with a female client who was complaining that her husband was always grumpy, always critical of her and the kids. She said everything would be fine in the house—kids playing nicely, everybody was happy—but when her husband would come home at six o'clock, things went straight downhill.

She said that she'd come to dread the sound of his key in the door because he'd come in, throw down his briefcase and piles of papers and lunch box, and the whole vibe in the house would go from relaxed to tense. She said the kids would immediately head downstairs to avoid him, because if they didn't, he'd immediately start barking at them to clean up their toys or whatever. She said she'd gotten to the point where she could just feel her body tense up, and she felt herself pulling away from him and his increasingly critical, unpleasant behavior.

When I was speaking with this woman, she definitely had some legitimate complaints about her husband's behavior. He did sound quite critical and short-tempered. I didn't blame her or the kids for wanting to put some distance between themselves and him. Still, this session with her and not him, so I asked her to describe her behavior and how they tended to interact when he came home.

"What are you usually doing when he comes home?" I asked.

"I'm usually cooking supper," she said. "Sometimes he comes into the kitchen to say hi, but usually he just goes straight into the home office to finish some files from work. He couldn't be bothered to talk to me or the kids. Which is fine with me, since anything he says is ignorant anyway."

"Okay, then I have a challenge for you," I told her. "Tomorrow, ten minutes before your husband is supposed to be home, make the kids pick up their toys. Then keep an eye open for his car on the driveway. When he pulls up, unlock the door for him and greet him there. Get the kids to help him with his briefcase and stuff so he isn't dropping things all over the floor. Welcome him home. Make him feel like he's the most important person in the world, and that you've all been waiting for him to come home because you can't wait to see him."

To this day, I remember the look on this woman's face. Shock, yes, but also a little bit of indignation. A little bit of, *"Why should I? He's the miserable one, not me!"*

Except that, in this case, the husband wasn't the only miserable one. They were both doing a lot of the same things—deliberately withholding affection, being stubborn and only seeing things from their own point of view—and neither one was going to be the first to soften.

You know what we call this, right? We call this a pissing contest. It's where two people are in conflict, but each is waiting for other person to take the first step toward making things better. We do this out of pride or pain, sure, but we also do it because we haven't stopped to look at our own behavior and how that is influencing our partner's behavior. We haven't looked at the whole stimulus-response cycle.

I'm happy to say that this wife did accept my challenge. She chose to let go of some of her stubbornness and self-focus, and instead she chose to make some changes—unilateral changes. That is, they were all initiated by her. She had the kids pick up their toys before their dad got home. She and the kids unlocked the door for him and greeted him there with hugs and kisses. At which point, it was his turn to be shocked.

There were no toys on the floor, so he couldn't complain about that. His briefcase and papers didn't fall over the floor, so that irritation didn't happen. In fact, instead of feeling irritated, he felt grateful and kind of touched when his family was there to help him out. So that stimulus of having his kids and wife help him out, sparked a different response—happiness.

Unlike most days when he was greeted by silence or coldness, on this day he was greeted with a warm welcome and affection. And that different stimulus sparked a different response.

Instead of barking at his kids, instead of disappearing into his office angrily assuming that nobody cared whether he was home or not, he actually engaged with his wife and kids. He felt loved and appreciated, and when he felt that way, when he felt that stimulus, he responded in a loving and appreciative way.

He asked his kids about school and showed interest in their day. He asked his wife if he could help with supper, and he thanked her for making it. The interactions between this husband and wife, and their kids, had changed for the better.

And the change was initiated by one spouse. When the wife chose to change and control her own behavior, she prompted a change in her husband's behavior. In fact, she prompted many changes in the dynamics in her home—that's the ripple effect. A single pebble (that's you, in this metaphor!) can cause positive changes to continue to spread out.

Now, think about it. This improvement happened without any kind of big talk or finger-pointing between these spouses. Instead, one of them simply took the lead and made a very doable change, which in turn prompted a change in their spouse, which in turn changed the dynamics, and feelings, in the marriage.

So by all means, think of your marriage as a type of machine. It has a lot of moving parts, that's for sure. By pressing the right buttons and flipping the right switches, you have the power to make it respond in the ways you want it to. That's the power of unilateral action and unilateral change.

What You Should STOP Doing Immediately

The truth is, nothing influences the interactions between two people as much as their respective personality traits and related behaviors. If your marriage were a battle zone—and maybe it feels like it some days—unpleasant personality traits and behaviors are the first things you should look at, as they are likely sabotaging your efforts to make peace.

In my capacity as a divorce and couples' mediator, I've dealt with higher-conflict personality types, as well as people who just had unpleasant personality traits or habits. I suppose some of these unpleasant traits are in our DNA, while we take on others as life goes on and we react, adapt, to various experiences.

Some people are fully aware of their more unflattering personality traits and do a good job of managing them: they realize they must do this if they wish to maintain quality long-term relationships in their life. Other people are less aware and do a terrible job of managing them. They struggle in relationships and may wonder why. Or perhaps part of them suspects "it's me" but they haven't really examined that further.

Regardless, some personality traits and their related behaviors are so strongly associated with unhappy marriages, and ultimately divorce, that every single spouse, whether the marriage is struggling or not, should be aware of them.

I'm going to present a number of these particularly problematic personality traits and behaviors here. These are things that are guaranteed to break down a marriage. These are things I want you to stop doing right now.

If there is a chance, even a remote chance, that any of your less flattering personality traits and behaviors are contributing to the negative interactions between you and your spouse, we need to know that.

Keep in mind that the goal here is not to blame you for all the marriage problems or put all the responsibility for improving the marriage on you. Rather, the goal is to gain insight into the interactions between you and your spouse, so that the marriage can be a happier one for both of you. Being able to recognize the negative personality traits and behaviors that you bring into the marriage gives you an incredible amount of power: the power to immediately reduce some of the unpleasant feelings and dynamics between you and your spouse simply by reducing the more unpleasant aspects of your own behavior.

None of us are perfect. We all bring less than stellar personal characteristics into our marriage. I encourage you to recognize yours. Take the lead. With a little luck, your spouse will notice your efforts and your unilateral changes, and will start to make efforts and changes of their own.

And if they don't do that on their own, don't panic—as we go through this book, we'll look at ways to deal with that. The change may start with you, but it will eventually involve both of you.

As we run through these personal qualities, remember that I'm not categorizing people or slapping a label on them in a clinical or psychological sense. This isn't about diagnosing a person as a certain personality "type." This is simply about being human and having some self-awareness and humility. It's about having common sense insight into our own character, personality traits, and behaviors, and about recognizing how those impact our long-term relationships. That's the kind of self-reflection we are all capable of doing and that we should all do from time to time, especially during times of marital conflict. One of the great things about this book format is that it lets you do this kind of self-reflection alone: that's when many people are most receptive to thinking about their own behavior.

I also want to make it clear that I'm not suggesting one gender behaves worse than the other. When I give examples of an undesirable trait, I might talk about either a husband or a wife who's doing it. That's just the luck of the draw. I see all of these behaviors displayed by wives and husbands, whether in heterosexual or same-sex marriages. People are people.

As you review these personal characteristics, I encourage you to remember that we all demonstrate some of these things from time to time; however, if I mention a certain trait or behavior and you think, "Oh, maybe I do that a little too much," then great—that's exactly what I hope will happen.

Because as I said, if you can make a change on your own, that change can reverberate in a larger sense in your marriage. Your spouse will notice it—spouses notice everything the other person does, especially when it's different!—so that gives you an opportunity to make a change and prompt your spouse to react to that in a positive way.

Yet some of this might be hard to read. I'm covering traits and behaviors that, if entrenched and severe enough, can lead to divorce—or at least a miserable marriage—and I speak bluntly about them. Remember your goal: to have a happier marriage, and to *not* be inadvertently sabotaging your chances for that.

Even if you don't think you display any of these unpleasant personality traits or behaviors as or after you read this section, you can still use this content to your benefit—take what I've included here as friendly reminders to actively behave in *opposite* ways in your marriage. That in itself can be helpful.

Finally, if I mention a certain trait or behavior and you think, "My spouse does that all the time!" just stay patient. I'll be talking about how to manage your partner's negative personality traits, attitudes and behaviors as we move on.

- **Self-centeredness**. This person, to be blunt, thinks the world revolves around them. They usually think their marriage and home life should revolve around them too, so their focus is almost exclusively on what they want to do. If presented with any kind of option—do you want to see this movie or that one, do you want this or that for supper—they will insist on their preference without a thought or concern for their spouse's preference. And if their spouse asserts themselves or disagrees, it's a fight. In fact, self-centered people often act insulted when their partner expresses a different preference. They may act wounded, as if their partner is only suggesting a different option to make them mad or somehow take their fun away.

Self-centered people are also **self-focused** people. If there's any kind of conflict or discussion going on, they only see if from their point of view. They don't stop to think about how their partner may think or feel about the situation: and even if they did stop to think about it, they wouldn't really care. After all, it's about them. They have a strong sense of entitlement.

They can also be self-indulgent. This means they're preoccupied with their own pleasure. They may say things or do things without a thought for how it will impact their partner. This might be anything from bringing home a pet without checking to making a major purchase to having an affair. It's all about what they want and what brings them pleasure.

• **Having a lack of empathy**. Empathy is the ability to put yourself in someone else's shoes. It's the ability to see, feel and process a situation in the way that that person does. It's more than just feeling bad for the person. It's about actually being able to feel what they are feeling.

Sometimes empathy comes from having gone through the same experience. You might have more empathy for a friend who just got laid-off their job if you've experienced a lay-off yourself. But you can also develop feelings of empathy by really trying to imagine what the other person might be feeling or thinking in a given situation.

Yet some people, and often self-centered people, often lack empathy. They don't have the ability or the motivation to put themselves in someone else's shoes. They can't or won't try to feel what their spouse is feeling, or to process a situation in the way that their spouse is processing it. I've seen some fairly extreme examples of this in practice. I remember a female client whose mother died. The husband was supportive for a few days as his wife grieved, but on about the fourth or fifth day, he said, and these were his words: "Maybe it's time to get over it. It's not like the two of you were close."

Nice, right? Now, it was true that this woman wasn't close to her mother. They had had an estranged relationship for years; however, that fact added even more complex emotion and grief to the situation as this woman had to make her peace with that.

Yet her husband lacked empathy—he didn't stop to imagine what it must be like for his wife to lose her mother when they were on bad terms, or to imagine what feelings or thoughts his wife must be having. He either didn't have the ability to do this, or he wasn't motivated enough to try and do this. Either way, it's hard to have a loving relationship with someone who can't or won't put themselves in your shoes.

But a lack of empathy doesn't just show itself in such heavy issues. I remember working with a couple where the wife basically made her husband the butt of every joke, and she almost always did this when they were out in public. Worse, the jokes for some reason were usually about his penis size. For example, they were having dinner with friends when one of their friends was talking about how he'd slammed his thumb in the trunk of his car, and about big and swollen it got. The wife ribbed her husband and loudly said, "Ah, that's what you should do! That'll solve our problems!"

The insinuation was obvious and it embarrassed the husband. He told her this afterward, but she didn't stop. She didn't stop to think about how it would feel to be sitting in a restaurant with friends, having a good time and relaxing, when suddenly the person you trusted most in the world blurted out a joke about the inadequate size of your genitals, so that everyone at the table could have a good laugh about that. Even though the husband asked her to stop making these kinds of jokes, they continued, and the marriage continued to deteriorate.

A lack of empathy can show up anywhere, so watch out for it. Take your spouse's feelings into consideration and always put yourself in their shoes.

• **Know-it-all behavior**. This is the person who thinks they know everything about everything. They are quick to jump into conversation to tell everyone else why they're wrong, and to enlighten everyone with their comprehensive knowledge of every subject under the sun.

Know-it-alls often come across as arrogant, grandiose and condescending. They will act like everybody else is stupid, and they will be intolerant of anyone else's opinion or input.

This is the person—let's say they're a chef by trade—who meets a physician at a dinner party, and who feels compelled to tell the physician all the things that modern medicine is doing wrong and why it's bogus.

In intimate relationships, know-it-alls are the type of partner who is constantly correcting their spouse, even when they're in public. They build themselves up by tearing others down, even if that means throwing their partner under the bus. Moreover, a know-it-all is like a dog with a bone when challenged or disagreed with. They react with an angry bark, their voices getting louder and more aggressive if the other person doesn't concede. Many people like this will actually lose their cool and storm off if the other person doesn't give in.

In a marriage situation, this causes very competitive and harsh feelings to develop between partners. It also causes a lot of pointless fact-based arguments, especially if both spouses have a touch of the know-it-all-in them (or if the other spouse is just tired of the behavior and has determined to fight fire with fire).

Picture a couple sitting on their couch watching a movie. Partner A points to the TV and says, "Hey, that's the same actor we saw in that sci-fi movie last weekend." Partner B says, "No it isn't. He was in that hospital TV show we used to watch." Partner A says, "No, he was in the movie." Partner B says, "No he was in the television show."

And so on and so forth, while—the whole time—voices are escalating and tempers are flaring over something as meaningless as what show some actor was in. This type of interaction usually ends with one spouse jumping up to search the movie database online to prove that they're right and their partner is wrong. But regardless, this couple's cozy movie night just took a nosedive.

Another habit of know-it-alls is to offer unsolicited advice or opinions. And typically, they'll offer this advice or opinion about something they have either no knowledge of or very limited knowledge of. You might call them the internet trolls of marriage.

A specific case springs to mind. It was a married couple who had two small kids: the wife was an accountant who had decided to put her career on hold to stay home with the kids, while the husband went off to work. Like many couples with small children, this couple was starting to drift apart. Life gets busy at this point and the kids can really take over. The husband was unhappy because his wife was falling asleep too early every night. She'd put the kids to bed at around eight-thirty and then she'd be out like a light by nine. And of course that left very little time for them as a couple.

Feeling frustrated, and understandably so, the husband began to offer his wife unsolicited advice about how she could better manage her day with the kids so that she'd be more awake at night. He told her in what order she should do the housework, how she could better organize the laundry and he told her that she should take a nap in the afternoon when the kids were down for their nap.

I remember saying to this man, "Your wife is a thirty-five year old woman. Can you see how telling another adult when they should take a nap might not be received too well?"

"Yeah," he said, "but I'm the one who's suffering because she's falling asleep so early."

"We're not talking about you right now," I reminded him. "We're talking about your wife. For all we know, that hour in the afternoon when the kids are napping is the only time she has to herself. Maybe she looks forward to that time, or maybe she needs that time to get everything else done."

"Well, if she followed my list she could get everything done and have a nap."

"Maybe she doesn't want to nap. Maybe she can't fall asleep during the day."

"Well, she should learn to. That would give her more time to spend with me."

You see how this works, right? You see how this person managed to make it all about them. Here, we have a spouse who was showing a few negative characteristics: self-centeredness, a lack of empathy and definitely know-it-all behavior.

Now, the lack of intimacy in this marriage was a problem and it did need to be addressed. But there are ways to handle a situation like this that are likely to work, and ways that are unlikely to work. And the husband's way—to swoop in with an air of superiority and tell her how she should do a better job of things—was unlikely to work. He had no idea what he was talking about. He had never spent a full day at home with both kids. Yet he knew it all.

The reason this case stands out so well in my mind is because the wife was displaying the same kind of behavior. Double the fun, right? Her husband was having problems at work with his boss—he was a mechanical engineer at some big plant—yet his wife had no reservations about telling him how he should handle things at work. She constantly offered unsolicited advice about how he should deal with his boss, or report his boss, or stand up to his boss, and so on. She constantly offered unsolicited advice on what he should do to improve production and get a promotion.

Now remember, she was an accountant who had only worked in an office setting, and he was an engineer who worked at a huge industrial plant. Their professional worlds were very different. She had no real-world knowledge of what he was facing, neither did she know the intricacies of his workplace or chain of command, yet every chance she got, she'd tell him how he could do a better job of things.

When it comes to the dynamics in a marriage, know-it-all behavior isn't just irritating and obnoxious, it's extremely damaging. It creates a vibe of animosity, competition and hostility in the home. That's what happened in this case.

Instead of offering each other support in meaningful ways, instead of brainstorming realistic solutions to problems, instead of working together and trying to truly understand the real-world challenges the other person faces, know-it-all partners just end up fighting each other tooth and nail for higher ground.

They waste massive amounts of time, energy and emotion trying to prove that they're smarter and know more than their partner. And every time they interact like this, they chip away a little more at their marriage.

• **Passing blame onto others**. This is the partner who dodges responsibility or accountability for their own attitudes or actions in the marriage by blaming their partner. This can happen in countless ways.

It's the spouse who has an affair, but who blames their spouse for their infidelity by saying, "You weren't having sex with me, so I had to get it somewhere." It's the spouse who overspends, but says, "Well, you're working all the time so I have to do something to make myself happy." It's the spouse who says, "I only yell because you don't listen to me."

You get it, right? This kind of behavior can really take its toll on the interactions between two people who are trying to build a life together. So don't do it. You're 100% responsible for your own behavior—every choice, every move, every word, every act.

• **Moralizing**. This is when a person believes that their values or ideas or lifestyle are morally superior to someone else's. Here's an example of this: A couple is sitting at their kitchen table talking about their thirteen-year-old son. He's a good kid, but he's a little on the lazy side and his grades are slipping. They both want him to pull up his socks at school.

The husband says, "If he doesn't bring his math grade up from a B- to an A- by the next report card, I'm going to take away all his video games for a month."

The wife says, "I don't think we should handle it like that. I think we should tell him that if he brings up his grade, we'll buy him a new bike."

"That's basically bribing him," the husband says. "We shouldn't have to bribe him to get him to do better in school."

"It isn't bribing him," the wife responds. "It's just encouraging him. It's something he can work toward. That's how I was raised. If we did well in school, we were rewarded."

"Well, that isn't how I was raised," says the husband. "I was raised to work hard, no matter what. I didn't get a new toy every time I did something I was supposed to do anyway."

You see where this interaction is headed, right? South. Because now, instead of focusing on how they can get their son to improve his grades, they've meandered off topic and started moralizing about which one of them was raised better!

Moralizing is extremely common behavior. Let's face it, we all think our values and lifestyle are the way go. That's why we live the way we do. But that's also why it's such a hard habit to break.

Let's stay one spouse is lying on the couch watching TV. The other spouse is irritated by this, since it seems like that's all their partner does these days. They just watch TV. And that's leading to a bit of distance between them.

A person who tends to moralize will likely address this problem by saying something like, "All you do is watch TV. It's like you have no interest in real life. I'm the type of person that likes to get out and do things, not just lie around."

The insinuation, of course, is that the partner on the couch is boring and uninterested in life, while the other spouse is the one that has true zest for life.

It's unlikely that this moralizing approach is going to help this couple focus on the real issue or work through it. It's more likely that the partner on the couch is just going to be offended and they'll end up arguing. So watch out for moralizing behavior. We all do it, but it can really cause some divisive interactions between spouses.

• **Having a critical spirit**. This is the spouse who always has something to say, and it's always critical, contemptuous or condescending. Nothing is ever good enough for this person, and nobody can live up to their lofty standards.

If their partner washes the dishes, they'll say, "You didn't rinse out the sink when you were done." If their partner is listening to music, they'll say, "How you can you listen to that awful music? You have the worst taste." This can create a miserable mood in a marriage, where one spouse comes to dread anything their partner has to say. Critical partners often criticize their spouse, both in private and in public. Interestingly enough, the more critical a person is of others, the less they are typically able to accept any criticism directed at themselves.

• **Defensiveness.** A defensive person is one who resists hearing any criticism about their behavior, even if that criticism is expressed gently, fairly and with respect. Instead of thinking about it, they immediately defend their behavior. Typically, these kinds of people are very reactive. They may get angry and walk away, they may say something rude, or they may pass blame onto someone else. They may start to explain or justify their behavior, or point out how the other person's behavior is wrong or just as bad.

They may do any of these things—what they *don't* do, however, is actually listen to or try to understand the other person's feelings, thoughts or opinions. They see any complaints or feedback as a personal attack, and they respond accordingly. The result is a marriage full of unspoken resentment and angry interactions.

I see this with clients, but I also see it in a larger sense. Let's say I'm on a radio show talking about common marriage problems. I might mention one or two negative behaviors I see people do, and it just so happens I use examples of husbands doing these things—maybe that's on my mind because I've seen those cases lately. Almost immediately, the studio phone will ring and someone will complain that I'm a man-hater. So I'll give another example of a negative behavior I've seen a wife do. And guess what? The phone will ring and someone will complain that I'm a misogynist. I mean, you can't win when people are this reactive and defensive, and when their vision of issues is this self-focused and narrow.

Not only does it make people with these traits or tendencies fairly unlikable, it also makes it impossible to have any kind of insightful, reciprocal or purposeful conversation with them. Talking to a very defensive person is like talking to an exposed nerve—there's not much thought process going on, but there's a lot of reactivity. Please, self-check for this behavior because it is rampant nowadays, both in our society and in marriages. And if you're doing it, you're making it impossible for your spouse to connect with you.

Many defensive partners have a habit of assuming that their spouse's intentions are bad—they assume their partner is intentionally trying to hurt them or anger them or disrespect them in some way. Yet at the same time, they're quick to dismiss or justify their own bad behavior.

They might say, "Oh, I didn't mean to do that" or "I had no choice but to do that" or "my partner misinterpreted what I did." This allows the defensive person to feel morally superior to their spouse. They think, "I'm the one doing it right, my partner's the one doing it wrong." So just remember that: if your behavior isn't intentionally bad, it's unlikely your partner's behavior is intentionally bad. I suggest you cut them the same slack you cut yourself.

• **Having a short fuse.** You know that kid we've all seen at the grocery store, the one who throws a fit when Mom says she can't have a chocolate bar? Well, some adults do this, too. They throw the equivalent of an adult fit when they don't get their way. They might storm out of a room, get snippy, raise their voice or slam a cupboard. Regardless, it's a little fit.

This person has little patience for others and little control over their own emotions or reactions. Sometimes, they don't know how to soothe their short fuse, but other times, they just don't want to. They indulge their frustration and let it blow, often using their behavior to get their own way.

Again, talking to this person can be like talking an exposed nerve. They don't put thought into what's being said to them, they just react. When a spouse has poor self-control like this, they can sometimes create a situation where their partner and any kids in the home must tiptoe around them or walk on eggshells for fear of setting them off.

If you know you're guilty of this behavior and you're ready to take back control of your own emotions, I have some strategies to help you do that.

First, ask yourself a simple question: Why are you doing it? That is, are you doing it because you don't know how to handle frustration, stress or disappointment? Are you simply indulging yourself because that's the easiest thing to do? Are you doing it because that's what your parents did? Or are you deliberately doing it to get your own way? Is it the only way you know to express dissatisfaction or disagreement, or to express your worries or complaints?

Do some soul-searching. You know the answer.

The next thing I want you to think about is what kinds of emotions "trigger" your outbursts. That is, what lights the fuse?
Now, sometimes when I ask a client this question, they'll reply by saying, "I'm triggered when my wife spends too much money" or "I'm triggered when my husband ignores me."

But this isn't what I'm asking. This is just blaming your spouse for your outburst. It may be that your spouse spends too much money or ignores you, but that's not what I'm asking. What I'm asking is this: What emotions trigger your outbursts? What are you feeling when you lose your cool?

For example, take the case of a man who says he's triggered by his wife's spending. On closer examination, it turns out that this couple is in serious debt. When the wife overspends, the husband feels fearful—fearful that they're going to lose their house or vehicles. So the emotional trigger is fear. And that's a common one.

He may also feel unappreciated. It may be that he works very long hours to provide for the family, and his wife's frivolous spending makes him feel unappreciated.

Or, take the case of the wife who says she's triggered by her husband ignoring her. Whenever he looks at his phone or chooses to spend time with friends instead of her, she feels unloved and not prioritized.

She also feels fearful—her husband seems more interested in his phone and friends than her, and she worries he has lost his passion for her. So as you can see, it isn't our partner's behavior. It isn't their spending or the fact they look at their phone. Rather, it's the emotion that we feel.

This is an important distinction to make. Why? Because if you don't make this distinction then you will get in the habit of constantly blaming your spouse for *your* emotional outbursts. And that'll get you nowhere. It'll only make the interactions and dynamics in the marriage worse, while at the same time preventing you from gaining any real insight into your problems.

You must accept the fact that you are responsible for your own emotions, regardless of what your spouse does or doesn't do. You are in control—or *should* be in control—of your own emotions, no matter what. Even when you blow up, you're in control—you're choosing to do it. No one is forcing you to do it. It's all you, all the time.

That's why you need to know your emotional triggers and you need to know how to manage them. This will help you exert your self-control with more insight and consistency.

Common emotional triggers include feeling unappreciated, unheard, unloved, undesirable, fearful, misunderstood, rejected or not prioritized. These feelings are so unpleasant that they can trigger an equally unpleasant reaction in some people who don't know how to handle themselves in a better way.

Having better self-control takes a few things. It takes self-awareness and the humility to admit that it's a problem. It takes knowing that your lack of self-control is taking a toll on your marriage, and it takes a true desire to change. It takes accepting responsibility for your own behavior without trying to blame it on someone else. You are 100% responsible for your behavior.

It takes knowing your emotional triggers and having insight into your own behavior. If you can do this, you can talk to your partner about your problems in a more useful way so that you can get to the heart of the matter—you can build empathy and understanding, and foster collaboration. Doesn't that sound better than arguing and overreacting?

The right attitude is also key. You should be excited and happy about making this change to your personal behavior. This isn't a bad thing to do, it's a good thing to do. So bring that positive energy to it. Be proud of what you're trying to do. Lots of people say they want to change, but most people don't even try. If you're reading this book, you've already shown that you're a cut above. So don't stop now. Keep going.

I also encourage you to have a clear goal: to have more self-control and to show your spouse and kids that you can do that. To make a happier home for them. To make sure that you don't pass on to your children the burden of having to go through life with a short fuse or the inability to control their own emotions—because they're going to grow up to do exactly what you're doing.

If you can show more self-restraint, you will dramatically increase your children's chances of having successful long-term relationships as adults. When you think about it, these are some pretty fantastic and noble goals.

In addition to having the right attitude and a clear goal, improving your self-control also takes willpower and some planning. Many people find that spending a few moments in silent thought or meditation helps them feel grounded and stay grounded.

Once you know your emotional triggers, you can silently remind yourself that, even though you feel those things, you don't have to overreact to them. There are better ways to talk about and solve your problems as a couple. You have options.

Talking out loud also helps. There's something really powerful and effective about hearing our own voice. For that reason, I often encourage clients to sit in their car for a few moments before they go into their house at the end of the day and to remind themselves of their goals. Say them aloud.

Something else I recommend is to record yourself talking about your goals and your commitment to practice better self-control. This is something you can easily do using your phone. Talk about what it means to you, why you want to do it, and how it will improve your marriage and home life. Play this recording back a few times a day, even when you're not triggered or upset. It'll help keep you in the zone where you're focused on your goals and motivated to achieve them.

Also, be sure to use strong, affirming language when you talk to yourself or record yourself. Instead of saying, "I can't lose my cool!" say, "I don't lose my cool around my spouse and kids." Saying "I don't" sounds strong, more in control, than the somewhat weaker sounding "I can't."

Another tip is to make being a more in-control person part of your identity. You might say, "I'm not the type of person who loses it on my spouse or kids. I'm not that type of husband or wife."

Embrace self-control as a personality trait, as part of your character, instead of just a behavior. Try to be a more patient person in all areas of your life—your blood pressure will thank you for it!

Visualization can also help. Visualize a situation where you would typically lose control: now, mentally walk through a scenario where you maintain control in that situation. Think about how good it would feel to do that. Think about how liberating it would be to know that you control your emotions, they don't control you.

Similarly, mentally play back a situation where you lost your cool. Looking back, do you wish you could have a do-over? Imagine that do-over. Again, wouldn't it have felt good to have walked away from that situation knowing that you handled it...well...like an adult? Do it next time!

Improving self-control is definitely an achievable goal. But I want you to approach it as a work in progress. Don't expect perfection on day one. Expect that your progress will be two steps forward, one step back. That's okay. If you say, "I'm never going to do this again" and then you do—because you're human—you'll feel so disappointed that you'll lose hope and maybe motivation. So think long-term. Think of the big picture. Slowly but surely, paint a prettier one.

You can also give yourself a bit of challenge in terms of a timeline. You might say, "I want this summer to be fun and stress-free for my spouse and kids, so I'm going to work hard until then to make that happen."

In my practice, I've found that many people who lack self-control when interacting with their spouse, who blow up in anger or meltdown in tears, are often unhappy people in other areas of their life, and may have trouble expressing their interests in a more positive, sophisticated way. So take a holistic view of this. There's no doubt it will improve the dynamics in your marriage and in your life in a larger sense.

Remember that anger or explosive emotions don't just make life miserable. They also make it shorter. Anger is associated with heart disease and research has shown that angry people live shorter lives. The shorter the fuse, the shorter the life. That's not exactly a winning combination, is it? A short, angry life? I think a long, happy life sounds a lot better. So let's aim for that.

When it comes to short fuses, all kinds of dynamics can develop in a marriage. It may be that both partners have hot tempers. That is common. Or it may be that one partner blows up, while the other retreats or withdraws to "keep the peace," or simply because they're sick of the behavior and don't know what else to do.

If you're the one with the short fuse, I hope this discussion can help you start to manage it, which can in turn improve the interactions in your relationship(s). If you recognize it's a problem but feel you need more or different help to manage it, I advise you to seek out the appropriate resource, such as a mental health professional with experience in this area, as soon as possible.

If it's your spouse who has the short fuse, I hope this discussion has given you some insight into that and what steps they can take to manage it, or how you might help them start to do that, if they're open to it (and we'll talk more about this as the book proceeds); however, if the problem is more serious or entrenched in your marriage, I offer the same advice—seek help from the appropriate resource, be that a mental health professional, lawyer, police, or another resource. If left unmanaged, this behavior can become abusive, and such circumstances go beyond the scope of a book like this. Always be proactive and find the right help for your specific circumstances. And FYI, this goes for any issue in your relationship or topic in this book.

• **The silent treatment**. Most of us are familiar with this term. It's when one or both partners withdraw into angry, hurt or resentful silence.

They might walk around the house completely ignoring the other person, perhaps refusing to answer their questions or engage in any kind of meaningful interaction. People who do this don't blow up, at least not right away. Instead, they keep it all inside, letting the pressure and the tension in the marriage build.

Yet the truth is, short-fuse behavior and the silent treatment aren't really as opposite as they might seem. Both can be used to try and control a situation when a person doesn't know how to do that in a better or more respectful way.

In some marriages, both partners have a habit of giving each other the cold shoulder. When arguments get too heated or they feel their partner isn't listening to them, they withdraw into silence. This is done for a few reasons, but often it's a way to punish or hurt their partner while at the same time maintaining a sense of control over the situation. I've seen cases where couples went for days without saying a single word to each other. Let's say the wife gives her husband the cold shoulder while passing him in the kitchen. The next thing you know, the husband walks of out the living room when she walks into it. And before you know it, both of them are trying to outdo each other—it's like a little battle...who can be colder and more distant? Who can outlast the other? Who can do a better job of acting like they don't care?

In other marriages, it's just one partner who tends to use the cold shoulder. Again this behavior is often a way to punish a spouse or to maintain control of a situation. If a person simply doesn't talk, if they just walk of the room and act like you're not there, they hold all the power—and in a healthy marriage, both spouses must share power equally. Yet by giving the cold shoulder, one partner gets to decide when, where and how communication can begin again.

It's like this: Let's say a couple is having an argument. The wife feels like her husband is criticizing her and dismissing what she has to say, so she stops talking. After a few more minutes, her husband notices that she hasn't said anything in a while, so he says, "What's wrong? Don't you have anything to say?"

She just shakes her head and walks away. So of course, he gets up to follow her. Before you know it, he's chasing her around the house, asking her what's wrong and asking her to talk. But the more he tries to get her to talk, the more she remains silent.

Well, this is an interesting turn of events, isn't it? She's managed to get him to stop criticizing her and being dismissive, and now she has his full attention. She likes that. She likes it so much, that she ups the ante and continues to remain silent until bedtime, not even saying goodnight to him. When they wake up in the morning, he pours her a cup of coffee and is extra sweet, but still, she says nothing. Why would she? She has him right where she wants him. She has control over him and over the situation. It's half control, half punishment and it feels good.

Do you do this? If so, you must stop. It creates a childish dynamic in a marriage. Plus, any behavior that seeks to control, whether it's loud or silent, injures the healthy balance of power in a marriage and creates a deep resentment in the other spouse. You might meet your immediate objective—to get your partner to fall into line—but you'd hate to know the thoughts and feelings they're having about you when you behave like this. This doesn't increase the love your partner has for you. It chips away at it.

So self-check for this behavior. If you're doing it, you'll find the strategies in this book will probably work better for you and give you true empowerment in your marriage, instead of just a phony feeling of being in control when you really aren't. But meanwhile, try to stop doing this. Remind yourself that the sense of power or control you get when you give your partner the cold shoulder is artificial and that this behavior is causing your spouse to have some fairly unpleasant thoughts and feelings about you.

Remind yourself that your partner and you are in this together. Yes, your spouse may be exhibiting some nasty behavior of their own, but that doesn't mean you should make the situation worse by responding with your own unpleasant behavior. Why make a bad situation even worse?

If your partner is doing this, I'll give you some tips to help you manage this kind of behavior later in the book. Right now, the focus is on becoming more aware of your own behavior and how it is contributing to the negative interactions between you and your spouse.

• **Micro-managing**. If you think being micro-managed by your boss is irritating, just try being micro-managed by your spouse! This is the spouse who, if their partner is out with friends or running errands, will text them constantly to ask them what they're doing, where they are or when they'll be home. This creates a home life and marriage where one partner constantly feels bombarded by their spouse's demands and requests.

Texting isn't the only way this happens. It might be that a person has found a few precious minutes in their day to watch a favorite TV show or play video games but, once their spouse sees them at leisure, asks them to do something.

It might be that a person has just finished putting away three giant loads of laundry when their spouse comes along and says they folded the towels wrong. You get the idea. As with all other behaviors, spouses have their own reasons for doing this— sometimes its frustration or fear, sometimes its manipulation and control. But whatever the reason, it has to stop.

• **Excessive or inappropriate sarcasm**. Now, I have to be honest: I'm a fan of sarcasm. I think it's funny and I think it can be a very effective way to communicate at times. But all sarcasm is not created equal. In a marriage situation, it sometimes happens that a spouse's use of sarcasm crosses the line from humor to meanness.

Picture this. One spouse goes into the fridge and takes out a piece of cake. They sit down to eat it, when the other spouse walks into the room and says, "Yeah, like you need that." The spouse with the cake then says, "That was mean." The sarcastic spouse then says, "Oh relax, I was just joking. Can't you take a joke?"

The tactic here is pretty obvious. The spouse is using sarcasm as a cover to say something mean to their partner. When their partner reacts in a hurt way, the sarcastic spouse can avoid responsibility for what they said by just accusing their partner of being over-sensitive. Watch yourself for this behavior. If you're doing it, you're creating a miserable and profoundly juvenile vibe in your own marriage. Mean sarcasm and a sarcastic voice tone always lead to resentful and ultimately contemptuous interactions between spouses. It's a direct path to divorce court.

• **Negativity**. This is the spouse who walks around with their head hanging low. They always have a sullen look or scowl on their face. They complain about everything and manage to suck the fun out of any and every moment.

If their spouse says, "Hey, that new sci-fi movie looks fun," they'll say, "I think it looks low-budget." If their spouse says, "That was a good meal, wasn't it?" They'll say, "Actually, mine was fairly bland." If you book a vacation, they'll make some dire prediction like, "It'll probably rain the whole time we're there."

Regardless of the situation, they'll find something pessimistic and negative to say about it. In a marriage situation, a chronically negative partner creates an environment of despair and hopelessness. They can be emotionally exhausting people to deal with, since their spouse and sometimes their kids are forever trying to cheer them up or put a smile on their face.

• **Super-sensitivity**. It's absolutely true that we all have different sensibilities and sensitivities. One person might laugh at a joke, while the next finds it offensive. One person might be able to handle criticism and shrug it off, while the next takes it to heart and thinks about it for days on end. Everybody is different. Spouses have different sensibilities and sensitivities, too, and we should definitely do our best to respect those.

Remember: don't be self-centered. Not everyone is going to react like you. They don't have to. Show empathy for your spouse.

That being said, we all need to be able to laugh at ourselves to some extent and to let some things slide, like water off a duck's back, as they say. There is such a thing as being too sensitive. This is the spouse who is immediately and profoundly offended by even the most gentle or warm-hearted ribbing. They'll react with shocked indignation and act deeply insulted, even if the joke was mild and good natured. And if someone has a slip of the tongue and says something even remotely inappropriate or politically incorrect, this person gasps with horror and judgment.

Sometimes, this comes from a place of self-centeredness or moralizing. Other times, it's controlling behavior. It can create a situation where everyone in the home has to tiptoe around the too-sensitive person. They have to walk on eggshells and choose each word carefully to avoid a reaction.

Your marriage, your home, is your and your spouse's sanctuary. It's the place you go to relax and retreat from the world. This is not the place you want to be displaying any extremes of off-putting behavior whether that's throwing a fit or retreating into wounded silence.

Always think about how your behavior is being seen and interpreted by your spouse and, if you have them, your kids. When the people you live with see your behavior, how do they react? Every action has a reaction. Always keep that stimulus-response cycle in mind and think about what interactions or dynamics in your marriage result because of it. That's what we're looking at here.

• **Divided loyalties**. This is the spouse who makes their partner feel like they have to compete for their love, time or support with such people as in-laws or ex-spouses. This is the spouse who allows their parents to say rude things to their partner, and when their partner complains, says, "Oh that's just my mom. She's like that."

As a result, their partner never feels like their spouse "has their back." Instead, they feel like their spouse is always taking someone else's side. While in-laws and ex-spouses often lead to feelings of divided loyalties, they can also develop when one spouse has an outside friendship (whether with a co-worker, new friend, ex-partner, neighbor, etc.) that becomes overly intimate and time consuming. This can seriously impact the interactions between spouses and lead to all kinds of assumptions and hurt feelings, not to mention affairs.

• **Laziness**. This is a pretty self-evident one. It's the person who just doesn't have the motivation to do what needs to be done, whether that's going online to pay bills, helping with housework, helping the kids with their homework, or whatever. Not only is laziness a very unappealing personality trait, it can create some nasty resentments in a marriage—that's because it undermines the very idea of two people working together in life to get the job done.

Here's an example. A couple is arguing because the house is always a mess. The wife doesn't seem to care, but it really bothers the husband. He finds it hard to relax when the dishes are piled up and there's laundry all over the floor. Instead of simply pitching in and helping, the wife says, "I don't care if the house is messy or not. It's more important to me to spend time with my kids than to have a clean house." Now, not only is the wife disregarding her husband's feelings and needs, but she's trying to justify her behavior by implying that it's morally superior to her husband's.

When it comes to housework, or anything else in life, frankly, the question is one of balance. It is possible to keep a reasonably clean home and still spend quality time with your children, but you have to work together, as a team, to make it happen. This wife let her laziness create some really nasty interactions between her and her husband. Not only did they end up fighting about housework, they ended up fighting about which one of them was being a better parent.

Another scenario I sometimes see happen is when one spouse is a stay-at-home parent and the other works outside the home. Let's say the wife stays home and the husband works. He comes home at six o'clock and, even though there's still work to be done around the house—cleaning up after supper, giving the kids a bath—he doesn't help.

Instead, he says, "My job is to work and make the money. Your job is to do everything around the house." It may be that their roles are pretty divided, and that's fair enough. But instead of pitching in and creating a team mentality in the family home, this husband justifies his laziness by falling back on these artificially rigid roles of breadwinner and homemaker. That's just not something that's going to fly in most 21st century homes.

Sure, we all get lazy now and then. That's okay. Just make sure it doesn't become a habit or that you're letting chronic laziness cost you your marriage.

• **Rudeness**. This describes a range of behavior. Sometimes it's just forgetting to use our manners. We stop saying, "Please pass the salt" and just say "Gimme the salt." We stop saying, "Thank you for remembering to pick up my jacket from the dry cleaners," and instead say, "Did you hang up my jacket after you picked it up from the cleaners?"

Almost everyone in a long-term relationship starts doing this at some point and to some extent, but some are worse than others. So again, self-check. Are you forgetting to use basic manners in your marriage or home? If so, this is definitely contributing to some negative interactions.

Yet rude behavior can get a lot more unpleasant than just forgetting to say please or thank you. Here's the case that comes to my mind. The wife was a fairly high-powered lawyer and her husband was a construction supervisor. They had been fighting to get along for better part of five or six years before I met with either of them.

When I sat down with the wife, she said, "I don't know why my husband is so upset. I'm just being honest with him."

"What's he upset about?" I asked.

She replied, "He thinks I'm rude."

So I asked why, what had she said that he took as rude, and this is what she said: "I told him that I was finding it hard to feel challenged by him, because he's not my intellectual equal. But I wasn't being rude. I was being honest. He's never been to university so it's just the truth. And we need to be honest with each other, right?"

Well, yes, we do need to be honest with each other. But we don't need to express that honesty in a rude or hurtful way. Most of us have known someone who shows a lot of puffy pride, you might even say arrogance, for their honesty. They might say, "I'm a tell-it-like-it-is kind of person. Either people can handle the truth, or they can't." But when people act like this, they're not being noble or forthright, they're just being rude. They have no tact, no manners, no social grace, and no humility. It is possible to be honest and yet do so in a way that respects the other person.

When comes to a marriage situation, it is absolutely essential to express honesty with tact and respect. After all, this is a long-term relationship. What you say to your spouse, and how you say it, is going to stick in their mind. They're going to remember it. Being honest doesn't give you a free pass to say mean or rude things to people. And frankly, some things just don't need to be said at all. So watch yourself for this kind of behavior.

• **Apathy.** An apathetic spouse is one who just doesn't seem to care. They're kind of checked out. They don't show much interest, concern or enthusiasm for their marriage and they don't seem motivated to improve their marriage. If their spouse makes a complaint or expresses a concern, they ignore it. If their spouse asks to talk, they just sit there and don't participate in the conversation. If their spouse asks them a question they just say, "I don't know."

As with many behaviors here, there may be any number of reasons why a person might act like this. Maybe they've been trying to express their own complaints or concerns for a long time, and they're just at the point of giving up. Maybe their spouse doesn't listen to them anyway. Or maybe they just don't really care about saving the marriage.

Apathy can also be a control thing. When you don't participate, when you don't answer your spouse's questions, you hold all the power instead of sharing it equally and respectfully with your spouse. You leave your spouse in a state of uncertainty and speculation, where they basically have to figure out what's going on with you and how to get through to you.

Self-check for this behavior. If you're doing it, ask yourself why? Apathy is a very contagious emotion. If you appear checked-out in your marriage, it's likely that your spouse is going to check-out at some point, too. And that is not a direction you want to move in.

Perhaps more than any other behavior, apathy is the one that most directly leads to marriage breakdown and divorce. Why? Because it creates a sense of hopelessness and indifference. It creates a sense of nothingness. There's nothing left of us. There's nothing left of the feelings we used to have for each other, good or bad. There's nothing left of our marriage. And when people feel like this, they tend to dial divorce lawyers.

• **Unreliability**. This is the spouse who says they'll cook dinner, but who, come seven o'clock, hasn't started anything. It's the spouse who says they'll pick up the kids, but forgets and leaves their partner scrambling. But unreliability can also be more serious and destructive in terms of the dynamics it creates in a marriage.

I remember a wife and mother of three kids who had to have a minor surgery. Her husband was supposed to drop off their kids at their grandparents' house and then pick up his wife at the hospital at four o'clock to take her home.

Now, in a strong marriage, the husband is going to be there early. Either that, or he's going to wait at the hospital the whole time she's in surgery. But not this husband. Four o'clock came and went, but he didn't show up. His wife, who had just gotten out of surgery, had to text him and call him, but he didn't answer.

Finally, she ended up calling their neighbor who actually went to their house and knocked on the door. As it happened, the husband had fallen asleep. When his wife reminded him that he was supposed to be there at four o'clock, he said, "Can't you take a taxi home? I'm exhausted. I had the kids until noon, you know."

As this woman was relating this story to me, she broke down in tears. I remember her saying that she knew—she just *knew*—that if something awful happened to her, if she had a stroke or got paralyzed, her husband wouldn't be there for her. She was equally afraid that if something happened to her he wouldn't be there for their children.

I talk to a lot of people in my line of work, and I especially talk to people who are sad or worried. Many are recovering from affairs. But this woman really stands apart. She was realizing that she couldn't rely on her husband and I just think there's no sadness quite like that. This marriage did end in divorce, by the way, which I think was the best choice for her.

That's because an unreliable spouse is no spouse at all. You simply cannot have a partnership with a person you can't rely on. You can't even have a decent co-worker relationship or friendship with a person you can't rely on, never mind a marriage!

Unreliable behavior creates both a vibe and a reality that are the exact opposite of everything a marriage should be. So if you know you're not the most reliable of people, if you know you don't follow through with promises, if you know that you let your partner down, you also need to know that this behavior is chipping away at the very foundation of your marriage.

• **Immaturity**. As with so many personality traits and behaviors here, immaturity expresses itself in different ways. Sometimes, it's just a product of youth or inexperience. It's someone who marries young and hasn't quite made the transition into married and family life. Yet a person who is old enough to get married and/or have kids is certainly old enough to behave as though they are married and/or have kids.

Excessive partying, disappearing for an entire weekend, staying out late every night or most nights…this isn't the kind of behavior that ages well.

Immature behavior isn't just for the young, either. Some people continue to behave in childish ways well into adulthood, middle age and beyond. We might think that name-calling, for example, would be limited to elementary and junior high school, but unfortunately, it isn't. I cannot tell you how many adult men and women I have heard basically call each other names. Mean-spirited teasing is another immature behavior that is all too common. Earlier, when I was talking about a lack of empathy, I mentioned a case where the wife consistently made jokes about the size of her husband's penis. That's the kind of thing I'm talking about here. It's immature and it's unnecessary.

Yet immature behavior isn't always mean behavior. Sometimes it shows up in the form of irresponsibility or recklessness. It's the spouse who overspends without a thought for rainy days, saying "We have to enjoy every day!" When their partner expresses any concern about finances, they just respond by saying, "Oh don't worry, the universe will take care of us!" or some such silliness. Please don't do this.

• **Thoughtlessness**. Some of the personality traits and behaviors I mention here are more or less conscious ones. People often know they're doing them. They often know when they're being self-centered or controlling or critical or rude or unreliable.

Often, it's a question of motivation—are they willing to acknowledge their flaws and work on them for the good of the marriage, or aren't they?

Thoughtlessness is a bit different, though. I've seen many people who were very much in love and very committed to the marriage, but who nonetheless were, or had become, quite thoughtless when it came to their spouse. When I talk about thoughtlessness in this context I mean it fairly literally—this is the spouse who simply doesn't think of their partner that much.

They've stopped doing all the little things for their spouse. They've stopped saving the last cup of coffee for them. They've stopped bringing home their partner's favorite magazine when they're out shopping. They've stopped surprising them with a romantic weekend or with flowers or with their favorite meal.

This is the type of thing that often happens in long-term relationships; however, once we stop doing the little things, once we stop being as thoughtful as we used to be, the dynamics in the marriage really do change, and not for the better.

So ask yourself: Do you think about your partner as much as you used to? Are you as thoughtful or conscientious of their feelings or preferences as you used to be? If not, is it possible that's at least partly responsible for some of the negative interactions that have developed in your marriage?

All right. These are some of the more common problematic personality traits that I see one or both partners displaying in struggling marriages. The way I've separated them here is in some ways artificial, since they may overlap. People may display elements of more than one.

For example, the husband who forgot to pick up his wife from the hospital following her surgery wasn't just unreliable, he was also self-centered, had no empathy, was lazy and apathetic.

More belligerent personality traits and behaviors may also overlap. A person who displays a short fuse may also be the type to be critical. You get the idea.

In terms of the marriage machine, these are the broken or at least rusty parts. These are the personality traits, attitudes and behaviors that cause the interactions between a husband and a wife to deteriorate. These are the things that make people want to get away from each other, sometimes for good.

Are you doing any of these? Like I said, almost everyone displays bits of these traits from time to time. We're only human—most of us have been defensive, or lazy, or sarcastic, or gone through periods where we weren't as patient, kind or communicative as we could have been. In long-term marriages, you're going to see the worst of someone, not just the best. We aren't striving for perfection, here. At the same time, we are striving to do better. Learning how to manage any unpleasant personality traits and behaviors that may be getting away from us is one of the first ways a spouse can start to do better.

Take a Look at This

You may see traces of your own personality traits or behaviors in several of the ones I've listed here, or perhaps just one two things really stand out. Either way, I have a little job for you to do. I want you to think about a time in your marriage when you acted in one of these ways—defensive, critical, too sarcastic, or rude. If you can't remember a specific incident, that's okay—you still know how you tend to act. That being the case, I want you to reproduce the experience all by yourself.

Go stand in front of a mirror and look at yourself. Make the same facial expressions you tend to make when you're exhibiting one of these personality traits. How do you look? Caring? Affectionate? Mature? Collaborative?

Speak aloud a few words that you might typically say when you're not at your finest. How do you sound? Respectful? Loving? Mature? Collaborative?

Probably not. You've heard the expression that a picture says a thousand words. That's why I often encourage clients to look in the mirror while they re-enact some of their worst behaviors. I want you to see what your spouse is seeing, and hear what they're hearing.

This little exercise can be a big wake-up call. Your facial expression, your voice tone, the words you choose—this is what your spouse is seeing and hearing, and it is directly influencing the way they feel and think about you, and how they react to you.

Now, look in the mirror and do a do-over. Reproduce the same interaction you just did, but this time force yourself to keep your expression and voice tone more pleasant, respectful, and collaborative. Which version of yourself makes you feel better about yourself? Which do you think would make your partner feel better about you and about your marriage?

Gadgets, Gadgets, Gadgets

When it comes to the interactions between spouses, when it comes to the dynamics or habits in their marriage, it isn't just negative personal characteristics that cause problems. Nowadays, another troublemaker is probably sitting at arm's length from you— your phone.

So many spouses complain about the damaging role of personal devices and technology in their marriage that this issue deserves a section of its own, here.

I can't tell you how many clients I've heard talk about how tired they are of having to compete with technology for their partner's time or attention. Here's a typical scenario.

A wife tells her husband, "I am so sick of seeing you walk around the house with your head down, always staring at your phone. It doesn't matter where you are, whether the bedroom or the bathroom, you have it with you. We can't watch a movie without you checking your text messages. We can't have a conversation without you looking at your phone. If you get a message during dinner, you have to answer it that second, even if the kids are in the middle of telling you something important."

"You're one to talk," the husband replies. "You can't go five minutes without posting something on social media. If we go out for supper, you have to take a picture of your meal and post it. And what happened when we went house-boating last summer? All you did was post pictures online. Don't you remember how you made me drive the boat around the lake until we found a spot where you could get service?"

Does any part of this sound familiar to you?

There's no doubt that the use of personal devices and technology is rampant in our society. And since this kind of technology developed so quickly, we didn't really have time to consciously figure out how we were going to incorporate all these gadgets, and the amazing things they can do, into our lives or homes. It just happened so fast that it kind of took over. That's why so many people just don't have that balance.

To make matters worse, personal technology is extremely habit-forming. Research is showing us just how habit-forming it is, and how people essentially go through a type of "withdrawal" when they don't have access to it.

You've probably felt that. I know I have. If I happen to forget my phone at home while I'm out and about, I have a distinct feeling of unease…that I'm missing something.

But that isn't right. And it should tell us something about how personal technology is infiltrating our lives.

Next time you're in a public place—standing in line at the grocery store or the movie theater, look around. Just take notice of how many people have their heads down, staring at that gadget in their hand. Next time you're at an outdoor event, whether it's sitting at the park with your kids or watching a soccer game, just take notice of how many people are staring at their phones instead of watching their kids or even watching an event that they paid a lot of money to see.

Next time you're out for dinner with your spouse, look around the restaurant and see how many couples out on their romantic date night aren't even interacting with each other. They're interacting with their phone. Now, unless one or both of them are world leaders or on-call heart surgeons, it's unlikely they need to be checking their messages or instantly responding to messages. It's more likely they can drop out for an hour or two and share a private meal with their sweetheart.

You need to know that when you look at your phone instead of looking into your partner's eyes, you send a definite message: this *ding*, this mindless bit of information or trivia, this co-worker who just sent a funny meme…this stuff and this person is way more important and interesting to me than you are. You're so boring and unimportant, in fact, that I don't even have to use my basic manners with you! I can just stare at this gadget and ignore you.

Look—I know that you and your spouse don't really feel that way about each other. But if you're compulsively or excessively on your phone or gadgets, it's very likely that this is how your behavior makes your spouse feel. It's rude, it's irritating and it's very hurtful.

Here's another thing to think about. It isn't bad enough that our use of personal devices and technology can be habit-forming and rude. To add to the drama, most of us become very defensive when it comes to our phones. We don't like it when somebody asks us who we're texting or what we're doing on it. We don't like it when somebody asks us to put it down or put it away.

So not only is one spouse irritated by having to ask their partner to put their phone down or away, but their partner is irritated by the request! They don't want to be told what to do. As a result, we have hurt and annoyance on one side, and defensiveness and annoyance on the other side.

You'll do your marriage a big favor by thinking about how the use of personal technology interrupts or otherwise affects the interactions between you and your spouse. Challenge that sense of urgency that tells you that you need to check your phone right now because someone might have messaged you or something might be happening. Most of the time, it can wait. Most of the time, the experience you're sharing with your spouse is more important.

Change the way you think about your phone. Turn the situation around: instead of feeling compelled to check it, think instead about how free you feel when you don't have to check it. Instead of seeing it as an act of sacrifice to leave your phone in the car's glovebox, see it as an act of liberation.

Put the phone away. Turn off the computer or tablet. Sign out of social media. Reconnect with the people you love and who love you. Because they probably miss you a lot. Rediscover your spouse and rediscover the world. Get curious and excited about these things again. Spend more time looking at your spouse and the world around you, and less time looking at a gadget.

A Bird's Eye View

Quite often, when I'm dealing with a spouse who is showing some unflattering behaviors but who is resistant to looking at those because their partner is behaving just as poorly, I'll present a little scenario, and it goes like this.

Imagine for a moment that I reach down from the skies and pluck you out of your home, out of your marriage, and I deposit you in another home, another marriage.

You don't know this new spouse; however, they're about your age and they're someone that you should by all accounts be compatible with in terms of values, appearance, lifestyle and so on. But you're complete and utter strangers.

Your instructions in this new marriage are to treat your new husband or wife in exactly the same ways that you're treating your real spouse now. You're to use the same voice tone, have the same level of patience and affection, and interact in all the same ways. Behave exactly as you behave now.

There's no being on your best behavior because you're just getting to know each other! Instead, you have to let it all show. All the worst parts of your personality and behavior, from outbursts and meltdowns to the silent treatment and staring at your phone. All if it.

Now let me ask you: How do you think this new spouse would react to you? What do you think they'd think or do when you behaved toward them the way you are currently behaving toward your spouse? Maybe they'd think they hit the jackpot! I hope so.

Or maybe they wouldn't think they were quite so lucky. Only you know for sure. Just keep in mind that familiarity and habit have a way of making us lose our objective perspective. We're so used to behaving the way we are and getting away with it that we lose the ability to step back, look at our behavior, and think, "Wow, actually, that's not very attractive."

Think about it. If you're exhibiting personality traits or behaviors that you wouldn't want a new romantic partner to see, then why in the world would you want your current spouse—who you love and who loves you—to see them?

What You Should START Doing Immediately

It's absolutely true that if you can reduce some of your negative personality traits and behaviors, you can reduce the number of negative interactions between you and your spouse.

That's what we've been focused on doing until this point. We've been focused on removing negative stimuli so that negative responses can't happen, or at least can't happen in the same way— and sometimes even that's a good start. It's pretty simple logic: If you're digging yourself into a hole, the first thing you should do is throw away the shovel! Stop performing the actions that are causing problems.

Now that we've done that essential groundwork, it's time to start building something on top of it. We'll do that by turning our focus to ways you can start *increasing* your positive personality traits and behaviors so that you can *increase* the number of positive interactions between you and your spouse. Positive stimuli, positive responses. It's time to start filling that hole back in and making your way back to the surface. It's a lot warmer and sunnier up there.

I said earlier that every relationship has its own vibe. I want you to change and improve your marriage vibe by putting out more positive and less negative vibes on a personal level. Take the lead in your marriage by having a better attitude and by behaving in better ways. This changes the overall vibe. It changes the dynamics in your marriage and the interactions between you and your spouse.

In my years of practice, I've found that all successful couples tend to display a number of the same personality traits, characteristics and habits. Some people come by these naturally. Others don't. They've had to make the choice to embrace these attitudes and behaviors, and they've had to commit to making them their new way of doing business in the marriage. And frankly, that's a pretty fantastic thing to do. Most people say they want to change, but they don't ever do it. By reading this far, you've already proved that you're willing to take steps to have a better life. So keep moving forward.

Here, I'm going to outline the personality traits and behaviors that tend to be associated with successful couples and happy marriages. If your marriage were a battle zone, these are the moves that would win you the war.

As you read through these, I want you to do some honest self-reflection—how good are you at showing these traits? How often do you behave in these ways? Maybe a lot. That's great. Maybe you need just a friendly reminder. That's good, too. That's why you're here.

• **Show humility**. I mention this one first, because nothing in this section is going to be possible unless and until you have humility. Simply put, humility is the ability and willingness to look at your own shortcomings.

In many ways, humility is the opposite of self-centeredness. People who have humility don't think or act like the world revolves around them. They don't assume that they know everything or that they know best. They respect their partner's opinions and feelings.

If their partner expresses a complaint or concern about the marriage, if their partner says that something is bothering them or asks them to stop doing something, they don't just dismiss it or blame their partner or tell them why they're wrong. Instead, they listen with an open mind and an open heart, and they seriously ask themselves if their partner might be right.

Plus, this person doesn't think they're better than their partner, even if they disagree on issues. Instead of moralizing, they are willing to admit that maybe they don't have all the answers.

In this way, this spouse is an easy person to live with. A pleasant person. The majority of interactions with this person are going to be respectful and collaborative when necessary.

Yet it can be hard to show humility—or at least to be the first in the marriage to show it—when the relationship is struggling or when there's a lot of negativity between you. A person kind of feels like they have to swallow their pride. They think, "Why should I admit I'm wrong? My spouse won't do it."

I get that. But guess what? That's exactly what can make a show of humility on your part all the more powerful and effective!

Your spouse still loves you very much, and when they see you bringing this kind of positive trait into your behavior and marriage, they will notice it. They will think about it.

And it is very, very likely that they will respond in a positive way. This might not happen instantly and it might not happen in the way you want it to. At first, they may say, "Ha! I knew I was right!" or "Ha, so you admit it!" But after a while, when their little puff of victory dissolves, they will reflect back on what you did and how you behaved, and they will feel love and appreciation for that. It is likely they will come to you and say so, and it is likely they will respond in kind.

• **Have empathy**. Again, this is the ability and the willingness to see, feel and process an experience in the way that your spouse might see, feel or process that experience. It's like this. Let's say a wife knows her husband has been working really hard for a job promotion at work. He's been putting in all kinds of extra hours and doing his best for months to impress the brass. Yet despite his best efforts, the job goes to a younger, even more ambitious candidate.

There's no doubt this wife will have sympathy for her husband. She'll say she's sorry that he didn't get the job, and she'll do her best to make him feel better. All that is good. It's good to feel sympathy when we see someone feeling sad or disappointed.

But let's say, not so long ago, the wife was also trying for a promotion at work. Yet despite all her efforts, the job went to a younger, more assertive candidate.

Now, the wife can do more than sympathize with what her husband is going through—now she can empathize. She knows what he's feeling because she's had the same feelings. She's felt the same anger and disappointment. She's felt the same sinking feeling in the pit of her stomach and the same sense of being passed over by her employer.

And because of that, she'll do more than just say "I'm sorry you didn't get the job" to her husband. Now, she'll be able to say, "I get it. I know you're feeling angry, sickened and let down. I know you're feeling betrayed by your boss for going with this new hotshot instead of with you. I know you're wondering whether you even want to work there anymore."

By showing her husband this kind of empathy, he feels more comforted by her and more connected to her. He knows that his wife "gets it" and that she's there for him. That strengthens the bond between them.

As importantly, having empathy gives the wife more patience and affection for her husband. If she only had sympathy, she might have thought, "Jeez, it's been two days and he's still moping around about that job." And when her husband caught that negative vibe, he would probably think she was being quite insensitive, and he might even start to resent her for that.

But since she has empathy, she knows that that sickening feeling in the pit of his stomach is going to stick around for a while. She knows the anger and hurt aren't going to go away that quickly. As a result, she is more supportive and their relationship gets stronger instead of weaker. The husband appreciates her support and patience, and his love for her grows instead of dwindles.

- **Get your priorities straight**. We all have a lot to balance in life: marriage, work, kids, extended family, home and housework, friends, hobbies, socializing, technology, down time and so on. Life's a balancing act. And sometimes we lose our balance. I want to share a little story with you: it's a common one so you may have heard it before, but it's simple and true, and it's worth repeating.

A teacher holds up an empty jar in front of her class. She sets four large rocks in the jar and then asks the children if the jar is full.

"Yes, they say, "The jar is full."

But then, the teacher adds some smaller rocks, some pebbles, to the jar. These fall down to fill in the spaces between the larger rocks. Again, the teacher asks, "Is the jar full?"

The kids smile at this trick. "Yes," they say, "Now it's full." But then the teacher takes a cup of sand and pours it into the jar. The sand cascades down to fill in the spaces between the pebbles.

"Now the jar is full," the teacher says, pushing the jar aside.

She then shows the class a *second* empty jar and pours a few cups of sand into it until it's full. Then, she tries to put a big rock into the jar—but of course it won't fit.

"The big rocks," she tells her class, "represent the big things in your life, like your family. The smaller rocks, the pebbles, represent other things, like work, friends and hobbies. The sand is the little things, the unimportant things that take so much of our time and energy. But here's the thing about life and jars—if you fill them with the little things first, there's no room for the bigger things."

This may be a grade-school exercise, but it teaches an adult life lesson. So ask yourself: What are the big things in your life? Are you putting them first?

A common theme in unhappy marriages is that one or both partners don't feel prioritized by their spouse. They feel that other things are more important to their spouse, whether other friends, hobbies, work, technology or entertainment. Think about how you can show your spouse that they are the most important person in your life. Think about how you can make them feel reassured that you love them more than anyone else, and that the life you're building together is your number one priority in life.

Just know that this takes more than talk. You can't say, "You're the most important thing to me" and then act in ways that don't support that. If you and your spouse haven't had a night out in months and a friend asks you to see a movie on Friday night, it's probably not the best choice to go with your friend. You should certainly prioritize quality time with your spouse over time with friends.

Yet this doesn't mean you have to spend all your time with your spouse. In fact, I'd advise against that. Friendships and outside interests are important in marriage. Again, it's a question of finding the right balance. Make sure those big rocks are in the jar first.

One way to show your spouse that they're a priority is to think of them first before you make plans or decisions. For example, if your friends ask you to go for a drink after work or to go shopping all day on Saturday, check with your spouse first. Call them and say, "Hey, I got invited to do this or that, so I'm just wondering if that works for you. Did you need me for anything?"

This isn't asking your spouse for permission. It's simply showing them that they're your priority. For all you know, something has come up on your spouse's end—maybe they have to work late and need you to watch the kids, maybe they're not feeling well, maybe the two of you were supposed to do something together, but it slipped your mind. A quick call shows them that they're front and center in your mind and that their needs, and your marriage, come first.

If you can do it this way, it's far more likely that your spouse is going to feel prioritized even when you are doing things with other people. They'll know that you thought of them first, and that can make all the difference. If you can interact like this with your spouse, if you can create this kind of cooperative spirit in your marriage where your spouse knows that they're your priority, you will avoid all manner of arguments and assumptions and hard feelings. Spouses who put each other first tend to have very strong and low-conflict partnerships.

• **Practice self-control**. This is the spouse who has self-restraint and the ability to control their own emotions and reactions, especially when things don't go their way. They're pleasant to live with. There's no need to tiptoe around this person or walk on eggshells. There's no need to dread this person's reaction during a disagreement.

This is the spouse who has the trust, love, admiration and true affection of their partner and children. This is the spouse I want you to be. But more importantly, this is the spouse your partner wants you to be.

Yet having self-control doesn't come naturally to all of us, and it doesn't always come easy. That's why I talked a little more extensively about it previously, under the discussion about short fuses. I encourage you to revisit that section or seek extra help if you're still struggling with this in your life and/or marriage.

• **Have an easygoing nature**. This is the spouse who lets most things roll off them, like that old expression "water off a duck's back." If their kid accidentally knocks over a glass of milk, they just help clean it up. If their spouse is having a bad day and is a bit more grumpy than usual, they just let it slide and don't take it to heart. If there's a sudden change in plans, they don't get mad or make a big deal about it. They just adapt and do what has to be done.

This is the spouse who would rather smile than frown. Who would rather offer a warm hug than a cold shoulder. Who would rather offer friendly support than criticism or judgment. Who easily forgives minor transgressions instead of holding a grudge. This spouse is a dream to live with. So ask yourself: Are you a pleasant person to live with?

A big part of having an easygoing nature is having the ability to practice self-control—that is, being able to choose how we're going to respond to something, instead of just reacting to any negative stimuli in a knee-jerk way. That's why I mention this personality trait after self-control. Spouses who interact with each other in easygoing ways, who aren't stressed by the little things and who can trust each other to respond to life's inevitable changes in predictable and appropriate ways, tend to have very happy marriages.

• **Be a whole person**. Too many people expect their marriage to complete them, and to fulfill every need. It can't. Your marriage is huge part of your life, the biggest part probably, but it isn't the only part, and it can't be.

It's essential that spouses have outside interests. Frankly, they'd be pretty boring people if they didn't! It's also essential that spouses take steps to find personal happiness and fulfillment in life beyond their marriage, whether that's with work, charities, hobbies or whatever. Take it upon yourself to be a whole person. Take care of yourself physically, emotionally, mentally and spiritually. Marriages work best when both spouses are happy, healthy individuals who have a life—and an interest in life—that extends beyond their marriage.

• **Have a self-sacrificing spirit**. Nowadays, we have this idea that we should never have to compromise or give up something we want for someone else. There's this idea that we should be able to have it all, and that if we have to give something up, we're being treated unfairly.

Well, that's ridiculous. The truth is, life's not always fair. It sometimes happens in marriage that one person may have to make a sacrifice for the other. If both you and your spouse have social plans on Saturday but your kids get sick, one of you is going to have to forfeit your plans and stay home with the kids. If you're struggling financially, one or both of you might have to sell something valuable, cherished, or fun, just to get by.

That's not a tragedy. It's just life. In successful marriages, spouses are willing to make personal sacrifices for the greater good. They're willing to go without or to miss out on a fun opportunity if that's what it takes, and they don't keep score or pout about it. Instead, they do it willingly. Spouses who are willing to self-sacrifice now and then understand the true nature of marriage. They have a mature and long-term vision of their life together.

They're selfless and, as a result, they can expect to win the love, appreciation and admiration of their partner and kids. And when you look at it like that, a spouse with a self-sacrificing spirit actually gains a lot more than they lose.

• **Show tact**. Tact is the ability to express yourself, including about sensitive issues, in a way that takes the feelings of others into consideration. Think back to the case of the lawyer who told her husband that she didn't feel challenged by him because he wasn't her intellectual equal. Well, despite this woman's intelligence, she had no tact.

If you have something to say to your spouse, if you have a complaint or concern to express, show some tact. Think before you speak. Don't assume that brutal honesty is always the best approach or that you can say anything, no matter how tactless, just because you're being honest or because you happen to think it's true. Use basic social grace when interacting with your spouse. Speak with tact and show some class. Your marriage will be a lot more sophisticated because of it.

• **Have perspective**. Picture this: A couple is arguing back and forth about money. Both are frustrated and their voices are getting louder. At a certain point, the wife throws her arms in the air and says, "I'm done! I want a divorce!" That doesn't help, does it? Don't treat every argument or issue—don't treat *any* argument or issue—like an apocalyptic event.

If you and your spouse are facing a problem, financial or otherwise, try to keep your perspective. Try not to think the world is ending and you'll be out on the street by the end of the week! People who overreact or worry excessively, people who don't have any perspective, can be exhausting to live with. If you're an anxious person and you need help getting this under better control, get that help. Your spouse will appreciate the level-headedness, and you'll benefit on many levels.

You must also have perspective in a larger sense. In a personal sense. Don't ever forget that your life as an individual has meaning, purpose and joy outside of your marriage. Your happiness and fulfillment as an individual walking this Earth are not dependent on your spouse or your marriage. When a person wraps their self-worth or happiness up in their marriage, they lose perspective. Don't do that. Yes, a happy marriage can make life happier, but it certainly isn't the only path to happiness, and you need to remember that.

• **Have a collaborative spirit**. A collaborative spouse is one who works with their partner instead of against them when trying to achieve a common goal.

Take the case of a couple that's trying to reduce their monthly spending. One option is for each of them to carpool to work instead of driving their cars. One spouse agrees, but the other says, "I don't want to. I like to listen to my music in the morning."

Another option is for them to bring lunches from home instead of eating at a restaurant every lunch hour. One spouse agrees, but the other says, "I don't want to. I like eating out at lunch. And I don't want to get up early every morning to make a lunch."

You get where I'm going with this, right? It's pretty hard to collaborate, to work together to achieve a common goal, when one person doesn't have a collaborative spirit. They just resist any suggestion that might cause them any amount of inconvenience or self-sacrifice. So don't be that spouse.

Instead, having a willingness to help. To cooperate and collaborate with your spouse to achieve those common goals. Instead of making it hard and resisting or making excuses, do what you can to make the process easier. Have a team approach to everything from finances to housework to parenting. Spouses who work together have marriages that work.

• **Look on the bright side**. A spouse who has a positive outlook is far more pleasant and easy to live with than one who has a negative outlook. Frankly, it's exhausting to live with someone who is negative about everything. It just takes way too much work to make this person happy, to constantly reassure them about things, or to make sure that everything is perfect for them.

So as much as possible, look on the bright side. When something happens, something bad or irritating or inconvenient, take the lead and do your best to approach it in a positive way. Not only will you create an environment where it's easier to manage the bad thing that's happened, you'll create wonderful dynamics and a great vibe in your marriage.

• **Have an appreciative spirit**. This is a big one. Whenever I'm working with an unhappy spouse, regardless of the specific issues that are going on, this person will almost always tell me that they don't feel appreciated by their partner. It's a constant and common complaint in almost all troubled or conflict-filled marriages.

So appreciate your partner. Show them gratitude for what they do, the big things and the little things. Show appreciation for the sacrifices they make. Praise them in front of your children so they can feel important and admired and invested in their own family unit. The more you show your spouse appreciation through words and gestures, the more you will prompt them to appreciate you.

At the same time, have gratitude for your marriage and life in a larger sense. There's an old saying: You don't appreciate what you have until it's gone. Maybe. But if you appreciate it now, you won't ever have to feel that kind of regret.

• **Speak in a pleasant tone of voice**. One of the easiest and most effective ways to create a "happy home" atmosphere and set the stage for friendly, affectionate interactions is to speak to your spouse in a respectful, loving tone of voice.

Watch for snarkiness. Watch for that edge of defensiveness, criticism, impatience or even contemptuousness that can slip into conversations when we're irked or distracted.

Speaking in a pleasant tone of voice is without a doubt one of the most powerful and practical things you can do on a daily basis to ensure that the interactions in your marriage and home life remain positive.

• **Have a long-term view of marriage**. Couples who are struggling often feel uncertain and insecure about the future of their marriage. They feel like they're on shaky ground and this can lead to some shaky interactions between them. Regardless of what's happening, let your partner know that you're in it for the long haul, so to speak. Reassure your partner that you love them and that you're committed to the marriage in the long-term.

This can really help stabilize the situation and create a sense of calmness, so that both spouses feel they can handle and ultimately overcome what's happening. This will lead to more stable and more calm interactions.

• **Have a curious nature**. Overcoming marriage problems requires something of a curious spirit: Why are we acting like this? Why are we struggling like this? Why is my partner unhappy? How can I make my partner happy?

People who are curious about things tend to have an open mind, and you're going to need that if you're going to understand your problems and overcome them.

So try to get curious about your spouse. Challenge yourself to see whether you can behave in ways that prompt more loving responses from them, and better interactions between both of you.

• **Be respectful.** Few things are as important in marriage as respectful interactions between spouses. In fact, respect is one of the foundational elements of a strong and successful marriage.

Remember that your spouse isn't just your husband or wife. They're a man or woman in their own right. They're more than just the person you live with. Remember that and respect that. Respect their interests, opinions, feelings and their freedom to be their own person. Respect their right to live in home that is pleasant and easygoing.

Remember to use respectful manners, too. Have empathy and use tact when talking to them, especially if you're talking about your marriage problems. Prioritize them in the ways that are reasonable with a marriage.

Respect your marriage in a larger sense, too. Keep your marriage problems private, and honor your marriage even when, especially when, you're going through hard times. Spouses who consistently treat each other and their marriage with respect foster a spirit of friendship and sophistication that can sustain them even through times of trouble.

• **Have passion for your spouse.** It's human nature—we all want to feel wanted. We want to know that our spouse loves us and desires us above everyone and everything else. So do that for your spouse. Make them feel loved and desired by you.

Not only can this improve the interactions between a couple, it can motivate them to stay committed to each other and work through problems when they arise.

• **Have and show maturity.** Maturity has less to do with age and more to do with one's personal character, the choices they make in life, and the ways in which they choose to treat others. Even when you're angry with your spouse, even when you're hurt or frustrated, never resort to name calling, character assassination, offensive profanity, goading or mean-spirited teasing. You're not schoolchildren on a playground, you're adults in a marriage situation.

Also strive to make mature choices, ones that reflect your circumstances and where you are in life. Living the single life was fine when you were single, but as I said earlier, this behavior doesn't age well. If you have a spouse and kids, it's time to act like you have a spouse and kids.

Adapt with maturity and grace to the changing phases of your life. After all, you brought these people into your life. Don't be a cliché.

• **Be fiercely loyal**. Successful, happy marriages are made of two people who are devoted to each other above all else, and they know it. They know that whatever insults and wrongs life throws at them, their spouse will always have their back.

I remember working with a couple who had been fighting to get along for the better part of a year. There weren't any major issues, such as infidelity, going on—it really was just a lot of nasty interactions between them, a lot of hurt feelings and assumptions and misunderstandings.

The husband came from a large and very influential family: nice people, but as usual, there was one who was a bit of a troublemaker. In this case, it was one of the husband' s female cousins. The wife often complained that when her husband was around, this lady was sweet as pie, but as soon as her husband wasn't around, this lady would make subtle comments about the wife being a gold digger.

I asked the husband how he tended to handle this, and he said that he would typically tell his wife that his cousin didn't mean anything by it or was just joking. That, or he'd suggest that his wife was being oversensitive. Regardless, he didn't do anything. He just let it slide.

I suggested that he handle things a bit differently and see what happened.

I said, "The next time you're at an event and your wife tells you this has happened, I want you to let your cousin know that you know. Don't make a scene, don't start a family feud, but let her know that you're aware of what's happening and you think she's full of it. This cousin of yours needs to see some loyalty and solidarity in action. More importantly, your wife needs to see it."

"But I'm not there when it happens," he said. "So how do I know what my cousin said?"

"Do you think your wife is lying?" I asked him.

"No," he said.

"Then why in the world wouldn't you back her up?" I asked. If one spouse can't trust the other to have their back, then what good is marriage?"

As it happened, the next event they were to attend was a wedding. At the reception, when the husband wasn't around, the cousin made some snide remark about the gold-digging wife. At the end of the evening, when everyone was saying good-bye, the husband put his arm around his wife. And then right in front of his cousin, in a very jovial way, he said, "Come on, my little gold digger, let's go home."

Now, by handling it this way, the husband and wife were able to present a united front to the cousin. But instead of making it a nasty confrontation, they chose to laugh at the cousin's insinuation and to treat it as absolutely absurd.

Yet the message was loud and clear: "My wife told me what you said, I have her back, and we both think you're full of it. So if you think you can be rude to my wife and not get called out, you're wrong. My loyalty is to her."

And as I suspected, this approach worked like a love charm. The wife was thrilled with her husband's show of loyalty and solidarity, and this was actually the turning point in their relationship. It changed the dynamics in their marriage for the better. There was more affection, more appreciation, more warmth and definitely more intimacy.

Always have your spouse's back! Be their loyal advocate, the one person that they know will always be there to defend them, to stand up for them and to stand beside them. Have fierce and unquestioning loyalty to them. Be the person that believes them and believes in them. Be that person in private, when it's just the two of you. But also be that person is public. Make sure you always have your spouse's back in all public situations, whether you're with friends, family or strangers. Let your spouse see your loyalty in action, and let the world see it, too.

If your spouse has done something wrong or something you don't agree with, it's okay to talk to them about it in the privacy of your own home. But your first reaction, and your public reaction, is to always have your spouse's back. I guarantee, they will love you for it and the interactions between you will be more loving.

• **Be thoughtful**. In the early days of a relationship, partners tend to be very thoughtful of each other. We remember when our partner has a dentist appointment and we are sure to call afterward to ask how it went. If we're picking up something for dinner, we remember how much they like a certain dessert and we make a point of looking for it. Yet as times goes on, we often stop doing "the little things" like this. This isn't always a deliberate or malicious thing. Quite often, we just become a bit too complacent and we start taking each other for granted.

My challenge to you, starting this moment, is to make sure you're doing "the little things" for your spouse. Make sure that you're being thoughtful and acting in thoughtful ways.

Pour them a cup of coffee in the morning. Set a glass of water on their nightstand at bedtime. Charge their phone if the battery is low. Fill their car up with fuel if it's running low or run it through the car wash if it's dirty. Look for the little things you can do and do them. These gestures, this attitude, can have a huge effect on the overall dynamics in a marriage. It's an easy way of saying, "You're always on my mind."

Keep It Simple: Like Attracts Like

You've heard of the law of attraction: basically, it's the idea that like attracts like. When you put out a certain energy or vibe, you'll get the same kind of energy or vibe back. If you put out positive things, you'll get positive things back. If you put out negative things, you'll get negative things back.

And honestly, isn't that exactly what we've been doing here? Like attracts like is one of those old concepts, those nuggets of wisdom and truth, that has been around for ages. Think of the proverb, "Smile, and the world smiles with you." Yet as with many simple things, people love to wrap it in fancy jargon or overlay some kind of special system over it. My advice is to keep it simple, and to keep the simple wisdom of that truth—like attracts like—in your mind and heart as you work through this book and your problems.

Remember Ralph Waldo Emerson's words. "*Love and you shall be loved. All love is mathematically just, as much as two sides of an algebraic equation.*"

Does this work all the time? Of course not. If one person has larger issues going on or ulterior motives, it won't work. But if often works, It usually works, especially in marriages where spouses are generally committed to each other and the partnership.

Got a Minute?

Okay, moving on from personality traits and behaviors now, I want to tell you about one of the simplest yet most powerful ways you can ensure that interactions between you and your spouse remain positive. And best of all, it only takes a minute—literally a minute!—to do this.

There are sixty seconds in your day that are pivotal in terms of how you and your spouse will relate to each other for the entire day and night. These sixty seconds happen in two blocks.

The first block is the thirty seconds when you and your spouse say your morning "good-byes" as one or both leave the house to go to work for the day. The second block is the thirty seconds when you and your spouse say your late-afternoon or evening "hellos" as one or both of you arrive back home at the end of the day.

The tone you set during these brief good-byes and hellos determines how both of you will think and feel about each other for the entire day and ultimately how you interact when you reconnect at the end of the day.

A spouse who says good-bye to their partner as they leave for work by embracing them, telling them to have a good day or remembering to wish them luck, whether it's for a work presentation or a dentist appointment, will have a partner who leaves the home with a smile on their face and feeling of love in their heart. A spouse who welcomes their partner home at the end of the day by meeting them at the door with a smile and a kiss, who remembers to ask how their work presentation or dentist appointment went, and who lets them know that they were truly missed, will have a partner who enters the home with a smile on their face and a feeling of love in their heart. The feeling is only enhanced if the person's children are also encouraged to greet them at the door.

Compare that to what happens in many homes: spouses who leave the house without bothering to say good-bye, and who come home at the end of a long, hard day to a house where no one comes to meet them at the door or even seems to notice or care that they are home. What house and spouse would you rather come home to?

Those sixty seconds can determine whether you and your spouse think happy, positive, loving thoughts about each other all day, or whether you have negative or apathetic thoughts about each other. It will determine whether you and your spouse look forward to seeing each other all day or whether you dread going home. It will determine whether your evening is spent in laughter, good humor and happy companionship, or in bitterness and indifference.

So take the lead and make the most out of that one great big minute of time.

<u>Warming Relations</u>

Because it's so important for you and your spouse to feel more loving toward each other as quickly as possible, I want to talk about a couple more things you can do, on your own if necessary, to improve your marriage before venturing on to parts two and three of this book.

When you and your spouse were "new," you were interested in and curious about the other person. You wanted to learn and know everything you could about them and their history: where they grew up, went to school, vacationed as a kid, and so on. Yet as time goes on and we settle back into our knowledge of our spouse, we sometimes settle into a kind of apathy, too, where we stop showing interest or curiosity in them, and in their life, in the same way. And both spouses feel it.

But as with so many dynamics and interactions, we can reverse the process. We can turn cool and negative thoughts, feelings, and interactions into warmer and more positive ones.

One super easy way to do this is to start asking your spouse more questions about themselves. Show more interest in them and in their life, both past and present.

When it comes to your spouse's past and their history, there is a simple little exercise I often encourage clients and readers to do. Sit down with your spouse—a nice glass of wine or cup of tea in hand—light a candle for a little atmosphere, and fire up your laptop or tablet. Using the street view feature of Google maps, zero in on the town or city where your spouse was born or spent their early childhood.

Ask your spouse to take you a virtual trip down memory lane…to navigate to the hospital where they were born, the house where they lived as a kid, or where their grandparents lived. Have them virtually walk down the street where they went to school, or where their best friend lived. Let them take you to the place where they had their first job, or where they went to the movies or rode their bike.

Don't rush the journey. Let them wander here and there as the memories come, and as they share those memories with you, their sweetheart.

When the time is right, journey to those places that have meaning to you as a couple. Where you met. The hospital where your kids were born. Where you took your honeymoon or went on your best-ever vacation. Where you almost got robbed in New York City, or where you had that great potato pizza in Rome. The first house you owned or the first apartment you lived in.

Nostalgia is a powerful force. Sometimes, when we're reminded of just how quickly time passes, and those who have already passed, it makes us cling a little more tightly to those we are still fortunate enough to share our life with.

This exercise—this *experience*—can strengthen the roots of your relationship and remind you that you love each other. It can warm the relations between you. I really hope you will try it when you feel the timing and mood is right.

The Bedroom…

Perhaps the pivotal interaction in a marriage is the balance between emotional and sexual intimacy. Couples who are happy outside the bedroom tend to be happier inside the bedroom. And vice-versa. That's why it's good to maintain both, even when you're having problems in your marriage.

Yet too many couples who are in conflict get caught up in a "What comes first, the chicken or the egg?" debate. That is, they can't agree on whether emotional or sexual intimacy should come first. I've dealt with unhappy couples where one spouse said, "I can't have sex with my partner until I feel more love for them." And then I've had the other spouse say, "I can't feel love for my partner until they have sex with me."

Not only is this debate a vicious circle, it's a pointless waste of time and energy that's only guaranteed to do one thing—delay both emotional and sexual intimacy.

Although this is a complicated and personal issue that may have many variables to consider, and while you must always do what is right for you, I'll give you my very general take on things: if your marriage is having problems and your partner still wants to have sex, and if you're either indifferent to that or okay with that (that is, you feel emotionally connected enough to do it), then go for it. In the absence of a reason to not have sex, then it's probably wise to keep that side of your intimacy alive. Many couples find they are able to work through some fairly serious areas of conflict without ever missing a beat in the bedroom. They continue to feel love and desire for each other. Their emotional intimacy and sexual intimacy remain pretty balanced.

Yet some spouses lose the desire to have sex when they're having marriage problems. It often depends on the type of conflict we're dealing with. Some types of conflict chip away at emotional intimacy more than others.

For example, a spouse may not want to have sex with a partner who is showing controlling, self-centered or untrustworthy behavior. They aren't withholding sex to punish their partner or make matters worse. Rather, they're withholding sex because the feelings aren't there. And if their partner is pressuring them for sex, it's likely the marriage is going to continue to deteriorate.

My thoughts, and my general rule—which you can follow or not—is this: when a married couple is in conflict, emotional intimacy should be present before sexual intimacy happens.

Why do I think this way? Because this approach is more likely to strengthen the marriage in the long run, thus leading to a good balance of emotional and sexual intimacy. It is certainly a better and more respectful approach than pressuring a spouse to have sex when they feel a lack of emotional intimacy in the marriage. It's certainly a better and more respectful approach than pouting when a spouse doesn't give in or withholding affection all the more, just to show a spouse how it feels to be rejected. These approaches aren't likely to improve matters.

Of course sex is important. It's very important. In fact, regular access to sex with a trusted, loving partner is one of the main reasons people marry; however, marriage does not mean that a wife or husband is obligated to share their body, especially during those times they feel a lack of emotional connection or warmth within the marriage.

If you find that the sexual intimacy in your marriage is beginning to weaken and your spouse is rejecting you or reluctant to engage in sex, focus on what is going on outside the bedroom, not just inside it. Are you avoiding those negative personality traits and behaviors that I covered earlier? Are you demonstrating those positive personality traits and behaviors that I covered? Review them. Live them.

Ask yourself, every day, these questions: How am I showing my spouse, today, that I love them and appreciate them? How am I showing my spouse, today, that I respect them and support them?

You should be able to answer those questions, to some extent, every single day. If you cannot, then I'm sorry, but you're not working hard enough.

You know your spouse best. You know what makes them tick. You know how to put a smile on your spouse's face and you know how to make their life a little bit easier every day, whether that's turning on the outside light before they get home or helping them clear off the table after supper. Challenge yourself to do those things. They don't sound sexy, but they build emotional intimacy, and that is the surest path to sexual intimacy. Strive to make your spouse happy and bring out the best in them. With luck, that will motivate them to make you happy and bring out the best in you. That's a great way to manage any marriage.

En Garde! From Unhealthy to Healthy Rivalry

While I'll be covering specific conflict resolution strategies in part three of this book, there is a concept I want to introduce here—although it isn't just useful as a conflict *resolution* strategy, but also as a conflict *prevention* or avoidance strategy. In fact, that's what this first part of the book is about—interacting in ways that prevent conflict from happening in the first place…and if conflict is already happening, it's about preventing it from escalating.

We've covered a lot of ways to do that here, but all of them revolve around the same axis: that's you, taking the lead in your marriage by embracing positive personality traits and behaviors. I therefore want to talk now about an overarching and destructive way of interacting that I often see in relationships, and what you can do to stop it the moment you feel it happening.

In some unhappy marriages, an "en garde" dynamic develops where spouses are always on guard and ready to fight. They are quick to essentially draw their metaphorical swords and clash, both competing with each other to have their needs or wants met, and to feel heard or understood or appreciated. They're in an unending marital swordfight, clashing against each other as they try to gain ground.

This competitiveness pops up in almost all areas of an unhappy couple's life and creates an unhealthy type of rivalry. You can hear it in the way they speak to each other. You can hear it even if they aren't speaking to each other! You can see it in the way they organize their days or plan even the simplest of events. It creates an atmosphere of antagonism in the way they parent, socialize, spend their money, and so on.

It also creates a constant, low level of resistance and contention that wreaks havoc on their emotional and sexual intimacy. It chips away at the foundation of their romantic partnership—they're always ready to clash about something, to draw their swords and start swinging. They're always ready to start fighting about anything and everything, anytime and anywhere. They're almost anticipating it.

Here's a typical scenario, one of a thousand ways in which this competitiveness might play out. Let's say on a certain Saturday a wife wants to go shopping with her sister. It's a rare day they can both find the time to go; however, this is also the same Saturday that the husband has a work golf tournament scheduled. Unfortunately, both of their kids are sick, so one of them has to stay home.

And that means the battle is on. Both spouses withdraw their metaphorical swords, adopt fighting stances, and start arguing.

The wife might say, "I haven't gone shopping for months with my sister. We never get to see each other anymore and this is the one day she has off work."

To that, the husband might reply, "The big boss is going to be at the tournament. I have to go. My job is more important than your shopping."

And then they're going to keep competing like this, waving their swords in the air at each other, until the battle turns into a war.

If this is even remotely familiar to you, you know that it has to change, and it has to change fast. And it can. You have that power.

The next time you feel yourself responding to that competitiveness, the next time you feel yourself triggered into an "en garde" emotional fighting stance or unhealthy rivalry, I want you to make a strategic withdrawal from battle. You can do this by remembering the importance of having humility, of taking the lead, and then doing something you might find hard to do—sheathe your metaphorical sword, step back, and let your spouse win the day. Concede, with love in your heart and a genuine smile on your face.

Here's how it looks in action. Let's say on a certain Saturday a wife wants to go shopping with her sister. It's a rare day they can both find the time to go. However, this is also the same Saturday that the husband has a work golf tournament scheduled. Unfortunately, both of their kids are sick, so one of them has to stay home.

The wife might say, "I was supposed to go shopping with my sister, but it's not a big deal. I know you're aiming for that promotion at work, so it's probably a good idea for you to make an appearance at the golf game. Anyway, you've been working hard lately. You need some sunshine."

To that, the husband might reply, "Yeah, but you never get to go shopping with your sister anymore. It's impossible for your schedules to gel. There's another golf game next weekend. I'll sign up for that one. It won't make a difference in the long run."

Do you notice the different feel and approach in this second scenario? Of course you do. The difference between the two is night and day. And the difference between these two marriages, and between the way these spouses feel and think about each other, is also night and day.

A strategic withdrawal isn't surrendering. It isn't giving in. Rather, it's creating an expectation within the marriage that any conflict or problem is going to be met with softness instead of with resistance. With self-sacrifice instead of competition. It creates a marriage where spouses interact as allies, not enemies.

Not only is the couple in this second scenario going to prevent a conflict from weakening their marriage, it's quite possible they'll both end up getting what they want anyway.

Because they're so focused on meeting each other's needs, they may collaborate to find a solution that works for both of them—they'll just make it work. Perhaps the husband will go golfing for the morning and afternoon, but come home right after the game instead of staying for drinks. That way, his wife will still have plenty of time for an early evening shop with her sister.

However, even if they can't make it work for both of them and has it to be one or the other, this couple is still going to come out ahead.

Let's say the husband goes golfing. In all likelihood, he's going to come home to his wife with flowers and pizza. He's going to thank her for staying home with their sick kids while he went out and had a fun day. His heart is going to swell with love for her. So no, she didn't get to go shopping. But she did just make her husband fall in love with her all over again.

If you can create this type of default interaction in your marriage, if you can compete to meet each other's needs and to make each other happy instead of competing to meet your own needs and make yourself happy, then victory will be yours.

This is a vital attitude and approach to have in a marriage—competing to make each other happy. This is healthy rivalry within marriage! This kind of marriage is going to be teeming with warm, loving, happy interactions.

Moreover, instead of having to resolve conflict after conflict, or talk through argument after argument, this couple will manage to sidestep the vast majority of conflicts and arguments they would otherwise have to face. So as much as you can, try to bring this way of interacting into your marriage.

As we move on to part two and eventually part three of this book, I encourage you to keep what you've learned here in part one in mind.

Now and then, take a few minutes to go back and flip through the pages to reinforce any insights and strategies you found particularly relevant or helpful, since they will slip your mind if you don't. As I said in the beginning of this book, the content you'll find within is cumulative, and you'll want to make sure you get the most out of it.

WORKING THROUGH IT, PART ONE

The Marriage Machine

Think of a typical or recurring negative interaction in your marriage. Is there a change you can make, on your own, that might prompt a change or changes in that dynamic?

How might your spouse respond to this?

What You Should STOP Doing Immediately

As or after you read this section, make a note of your less flattering personality traits or behaviors.

Why do you think you behave in these ways?

How might you work on improving these? Be specific and address each trait or behavior in turn.

If you were to improve these, how might that make you feel about yourself?

If you were to improve these, would your spouse notice? If so, how might they respond? Be specific and go through each trait and behavior in turn.

Gadgets, Gadgets, Gadgets

Are personal devices or personal technology, including social media, causing problems in your marriage? If so, how?

How might you prompt a change here?

What You Should START Doing Immediately

As or after you read this section, make a note of those traits or behaviors that you feel you need to practice more in your life.

How might improving these improve the interactions between you and your spouse? Be specific and address each trait or behavior in turn.

How might improving these improve the interactions you have with other people (e.g. co-workers, your children, your friends, etc.). Be specific and address each trait or behavior in turn.

Keep It Simple: Like Attracts Like

Can you think of a typical interaction or scenario where your negativity (whether in attitude, words or behavior) triggered a negative response in your spouse?

Now replay: Remember the above interaction or scenario, but imagine that you had instead put out some kind of positive energy (whether in attitude, words or behavior)…might your spouse's reaction have been different?

Challenge yourself: think of two or three scenarios in your daily life where you can inject this simple concept of "like attracts like" into your marriage and/or family life.

Got a Minute?

Regardless of your specific schedules, there is no doubt a time in the day when you and your spouse separate and then come back together (whether one or both of you go to work, or even to your respective home offices). What can you do to make these goings and comings more positive, and thus set a better tone?

Warming Relations

How can you show your spouse that you are still interested in them as a person?

Try the "Google street view" exercise in this section and see whether the power of nostalgia can rekindle feelings of warmth between you.

The Bedroom…

Do you think you have a good balance of emotional and physical intimacy in your marriage? If not, what part is lacking?

How can you improve the emotional intimacy in your marriage?

How can you improve the physical intimacy in your marriage?

How can you show your spouse, on a daily basis, that you appreciate them?

En Garde! From Unhealthy to Healthy Rivalry

Do you see the "en garde" dynamic in your marriage? If so, think of a specific example.

Replay the above example in your mind. What could you have done differently in that situation?

If you had conceded and focused on meeting your spouse's needs in that moment, what might have happened? That is, how might your spouse have responded?

How can you commit to meeting any conflict or problem in your marriage with softness and collaboration instead of hardness and resistance?

Think back to an argument or conflict when you and your spouse were competing to have your needs met. Replay it in your mind. What could you have done differently in that situation to show your spouse that you prioritized their needs, or were putting them above your own?

Had you prioritized your spouse's needs during that argument or conflict, how might they have responded?

Can you think of a situation where your spouse prioritized your needs over their own? If you can, express appreciation for that to your spouse—and then try to make this the way you approach conflict in the future.

PART TWO:

How to Talk About Anything: Purposeful, Painless Conversation

How Well Do You…?

In part one of this book, we covered a range of personality traits and behaviors, both good and bad, that can make or break a marriage. I challenged you to take the lead in your marriage and to behave in ways that are most likely to prompt positive changes in the way your spouse behaves. I talked about how essential it is for spouses to interact with affection, respect, appreciation, easygoingness and so on, and how important it is to nourish intimacy inside and outside the bedroom. I also challenged you to create that dynamic in your marriage where you're competing to fulfill each other's needs, instead of competing to have your own needs fulfilled.

Here in part two, I'm going to offer some fantastic and highly usable communication strategies, but I first want to remind you how this book works: all three parts work in unison, with each part building on the last.

I strongly believe—because I've seen it happen this way time and time again—that a couple who improves their interactions before talking about their relationship problems exponentially increases the chances of that conversation going well. Very well, in fact. Why? Because they actually have good feelings toward the person they're talking to!

It's common sense, isn't it? If you must have a heavy conversation with someone, do you want it to be with someone whose company you enjoy, somebody who shows up with pizza and a smile, or with someone whose miserable company makes you want to gnaw off your own leg to get away from them? Naturally, you'd rather talk to someone you like, who is easy to be around and who you have overall good feelings about, even during times of conflict.

I've worked with countless couples who can't communicate. This might be anything from a couple that's yelling and screaming at each other, to one that's completely shut down.

It might be a couple that's been shaken by an infidelity or that is struggling with any manner of marriage problems, from blended-family situations to midlife crises and everything in between. One partner might be belligerent, the other might be in tears. One might be very motivated to save the marriage, the other might already be checked out.

Yet despite the variety of issues, circumstances and personalities that I deal with, whenever I sit down for a mediation session with a new client, one of the first questions I ask is, "How well do you understand your partner?"

Some people will say, "Oh, very well," but within minutes of the consult starting, it becomes as clear to them as is it to me that they don't understand their partner nearly as well as they thought they did. Other people will admit off the bat that they don't understand their spouse. They'll just shrug and say, "They're a total mystery to me."

So why don't we understand our spouse as well as we think we do, or as at least as well as we should? The answer is simple. Because when spouses aren't communicating, when they're fighting to get along, they're both usually a lot more focused on trying to get their partner to understand them than to understand their partner. They put a lot more energy into expressing their own feelings, thoughts and perspectives than on understanding their partner's.

The result is two people who are talking, but not listening, and certainly not processing anything in an insightful way. They're either saying something about themselves, or they're waiting for their partner to stop talking so that they can say something about themselves. That's human nature. We all want to be heard. We all want to be understood. And when that doesn't happen, well, we try harder.

Some people get louder—I mean, that's natural when you don't feel heard, right? Other people get quieter: *You're not listening anyway, so I might as well just sit here and scream inside my own head...*"

There are many ways we react when we don't feel heard or understood, or when we don't feel that our emotions or opinions are being validated by our spouse. We get frustrated, and that's going to show one way or another.

Peace Talks: Diplomatic Discussions

It's a trait of human nature, for whatever reason, that we can't listen to what someone else says, we can't focus enough to understand or even care what they say or where they're coming from, unless and until they've listened to us first. We need to say our bit, we need to feel heard and understood, and we compete to do that. **We all have a built-in "let me go first" setting.**

This is why every formal body in the world, from the little brick courthouse in your community to the mighty United Nations, has strict rules regarding communication—who gets to talk, in what order, about what specifically, for how long, and under what constraints or conditions. And then there are more rules about how someone can respond to what that person said—how, when, what, for how long, and under what constraints or conditions. And then there are even more rules about how, when and what kinds of questions can be asked to delve deeper into the issue and bring more elements into the discussion.

If we didn't do it that way, chaos would reign supreme. We'd have UN delegates shouting at each other like angry spouses. That wouldn't do much for world peace, would it? We'd have peace-making delegates competing so hard to be heard that they'd probably start a war.

Yet private households don't have these kinds of clear cut and enforceable rules. I know some practitioners will try to reproduce the spirit of them to some extent by using a "talking stick" (which, by the way, is a traditional item used by indigenous people to keep order during communication). If this kind of thing works for you, great.

Personally, I'm not a huge fan of this approach, since I've found too many spouses just end up waiting for their turn, which again, goes against the spirit of true communication within the context of marriage. Two intimate people should be able to communicate without having to pass something between them or follow strict communication rules. True communication in marriage requires three things: a shift in thinking, a few simple communication skills, and the motivation to invoke those things.

As the spouse who is likely taking the lead, you must be the first to move away from an individualistic attitude. You have to stop focusing on proving why you're right and your partner is wrong. You have to stop focusing on laying blame or winning an argument or getting your way. You have to stop talking *ad nauseam*, trying desperately, maybe even angrily, to make your partner listen to you or understand you.

Instead, you have to start focusing on trying to understand your spouse. You have to get curious about why they're behaving in certain ways or saying certain things. As far I'm concerned, understanding our partner's feelings, thoughts and perspectives is step one when it comes to communicating in a way that is purposeful and painless.

Now, at this point, you might be thinking: *Okay, I'm willing to slow down and really focus on understanding my partner. But what about me? I want to be heard and understood, too.*

Of course you do. And you will be. In fact, my approach gives you the best chance of creating a mood and environment where your spouse will be willing to hear you with an open mind and an open heart.

Remember: people won't listen to you or care about what you have to say unless and until they feel you have listened to them and care about what they say. That's why too many conversations turn into arguments where two people are competing to speak, to be heard, and to be understood.

Remember the power of healthy rivalry. I want you to focus on hearing and understanding your partner. I want you to devote the time, emotion and energy to listening, to understanding, and to validating your partner. **You don't have to agree with everything they say, but you do have to go through this process.**

And when you've gone through this process, your spouse will be far more likely to devote the time, emotion and energy to listening, understanding and validating you. It's a straightforward approach. Let them get it all out, and make sure that you get it. And then it's your turn.

Now, some people will resist this approach. They've been fighting to get along for a long time and there's so much animosity and frustration that they're basically in a pissing contest with their partner. They think, why should I be the one to soften first? Why should I be the one to listen and care first? That's not fair.

Well, I can't make you do it. All I can tell you is that it works. When people say that something is "simple but not easy," they're talking about an approach like this. It's simple enough to grasp—put your partner first—but it's not easy to do when there's a history of frustration and hurt and anger.

Yet it needs to be done. We need to get up to that new, higher plateau where both of you are competing to put each other's needs first. That includes competing to hear and understand each other first. It also includes getting curious about your spouse: Why do they speak, feel or behave like they do?

Think back to part one and all those positive personality traits and behaviors I went through: humility, empathy, a collaborative spirit, having a long-term view of the marriage and so on. Why do you think I encouraged you to embrace those? Because you're going to need them here. So focus on your goal—to get along, and to be able to have a purposeful, even pleasant conversation. To feel like allies instead of enemies. To be that elderly couple walking along the beach hand in hand.

Peace Talks: Gathering Intelligence

Before any important event that involves speaking or communicating, a certain amount of prep work has to be done. Facts and intelligence have to be gathered. Think of a legal trial. Before a lawyer makes their opening or closing statement, before they ask a witness any questions, they do a lot of prep work. For every minute their mouth is open saying something, there's a day or more of prep work behind it.

The same thing goes for diplomats trying to reach an agreement or negotiate a peace treaty. They gather intelligence. They ask themselves a lot of questions. What does this other person or party want out of all of this? What are their complaints and grievances right now?

They ask these kinds of questions so that they can better understand the other side. That way, when they do sit down to discuss matters face to face, the conversation is going to be a much more purposeful and positive one.

They're already going to have insight and possibly even some empathy into their other side's perspectives, feelings and needs. They're able to anticipate a lot of what might be said, and they're able to be prepared with well thought out responses and comments.

Yet when it comes to communicating with our spouse, we don't do that. We usually don't do any kind of prep work at all. We just launch into a conversation or an accusation or a complaint or an argument or an assumption. And that's why so many conversations turn into such battle zones.

The most successful conversations, ones that actually make both spouses feel good and do good things for the marriage, take some prep work in the form of intelligence gathering.

They're successful because one or both spouses invested the time, emotion and energy to think about them in advance: that is, to think about their partner's perspectives, feelings and needs and to anticipate what complaints and goals their partner may have. They've done everything they can to make their partner feel understood, heard and validated.

Imagine this: a client calls me and says, "Deb, my husband won't talk to me. I know something is bothering him and I keep asking him what's wrong, but he won't say a word. I keep asking him to sit down and talk to me, but he won't. And that's not fair. If something is bothering him he should talk to me. I can't read his mind."

"Actually," I say, "You probably can read his mind. You've been married to this guy for over a decade. You know him very well. I'd bet, if you really sat down and thought about it, you'd be able to figure out what's bothering him. So think about. What has he complained about in the past? What kinds of things tend to bother him in your marriage or home life?"

So this client thinks about it. Instead of chasing her husband around the house and driving him nuts by asking him what's wrong, she sits down and starts gathering intelligence. And within five minutes, she has some pretty good ideas about what could be upsetting her husband.

For starters, he's been after the kids lately to put their electronics away. He's recently had to replace two tablets because they were left lying around to get knocked off tables and stepped on. He's constantly reminding the kids to pick them up and has asked his wife to also remind the kids, but it usually slips her mind.

So nothing has changed. Every time he goes into the living room, there's the new expensive tablet lying in the middle of the floor, just waiting to be stepped on.

On top of that, he's been trying to get the kids to do more chores around the house. He's asked them several times to pick up some fallen branches in the front yard and to mow the lawn, and he's asked his wife to stay on top of them about it.

However, when he comes home from work, the kids are playing with friends and the yardwork still hasn't been done.

So really, there was absolutely no reason for her to ask her husband what was bothering him. It was pretty obvious. He was irritated that the kids still hadn't done what was asked of them, and he was doubly irritated that his wife wasn't backing him up in terms of getting their kids to step up.

To make matters worse, it seemed to him that everybody was totally oblivious as to why he would be upset. It felt like nobody was listening to him or respecting his role as a father. He didn't feel heard, understood or validated by his family.

Remember that the purpose of communication is to gain understanding and to exchange information. This case is a great example of how that can sometimes happen without a single word being exchanged. This wife was able to look back at the interactions and conversations between her and her husband. And instead of launching into another pointless and redundant conversation, instead of asking him what was wrong, she decided to "communicate" with him in a different way.

She cleared some space on a bookshelf in the living room and told the kids that the tablet had to be put back there when they weren't using it. And then when they forgot yet again, she took it away and said they couldn't use it until the weekend. She also had the lawnmower ready and waiting for them when they got home from school, so that they could get the yardwork done before their dad came home.

And what a homecoming it was. The husband pulled into the driveway, saw the cleaned-up yard, and was smiling ear to ear before he even got out of the car.

Later, when his wife told him that she'd taken the tablet away until the weekend because the kids had left it on the floor again, he gave her a big hug and thanked her for backing him up and for staying on top of the kids when he wasn't there. He said that it made him feel like they were a team.

So as it turned out, the wife was a mind reader. Sort of. She knew her husband well enough to gather some intelligence and make an educated guess about what was bothering him. No further communication was required. In fact, further communication would only have made matters worse as the husband's frustration and sense of being ignored would only have been exacerbated. Instead of talking, the wife took the initiative and took steps to address those complaints her husband had already expressed.

If you and your spouse have been fighting to get along, I want you to use a similar strategy. Start by gathering intelligence. When it comes to conflict, what do you already know bothers your spouse? What do you suspect bothers your spouse? The more you know, the more you can make them feel heard, understood and validated. And the more your spouse feels that way, the more they will try to make you feel the way.

Plus, when it comes time to actually have a face to face conversation about your marriage or your complaints or problems, you'll be much better prepared to do that. You'll already have some insight and perspective. You'll already have something meaningful and relevant to contribute to the conversation. You won't have to start from scratch. You won't have to make your partner repeat the same complaints or concerns they've already repeated a thousand times. That's going to wear anyone down.

To help you do all of this, I'm going to present you with ten intelligence-gathering questions to ask yourself. Answer these questions to the best of your ability. If you don't know an answer, just speculate. Your best guess is fine. You know your partner better than anyone, so use that knowledge base to try and understand them and your problems in a more meaningful way.

These questions may seem superficial; however, once you start really thinking about them, they should take you to a deeper place. Use them as catalysts to get your mind going, so that you can gain insight into what's going on in your marriage.

1. What past complaints has my spouse expressed about me? Have they said I'm too critical, that I'm not supportive or that I overspend, have they said I'm lazy or not affectionate or always on the phone?

2. What past complaints has my spouse expressed about our marriage or our lifestyle? Are we too busy or disorganized, do we carry too much debt or is our house too messy? Do we have problems with an unhealthy diet or too much technology or a child-centered marriage?

Again, few couples are satisfied with every area of their marriage or lifestyle. We all have areas we want to improve. Think about those areas you know your spouse wants to improve.

3. Has my spouse asked me to do something or take some kind of action lately? Have I done it? If not, how might that be affecting my spouse?

This could be anything, really. It could be finishing a household chore or staying on budget or ending an opposite-sex friendship.

4. What complaints have I expressed to my spouse about them? Might my spouse be feeling unduly criticized, unloved or unappreciated?

Actually think about the specific complaints you've been expressing. Are some of them more legitimate or warranted than others?

5. Have I been taking the lead in my marriage to create positive interactions between my spouse and I?

6. Have I been putting effort into our emotional and sexual intimacy? Might my spouse be feeling unimportant, unloved or not prioritized?

Take some time to reflect on your intimacy or connection on a daily and nightly basis.

7. Have I been making my spouse feel appreciated?

Try to think of specific ways you've been expressing or showing appreciation. You might also want to think about a situation where you should have expressed or shown appreciation but didn't do so.

8. Have I been displaying any negative personality traits or behaviors lately?

To answer this question, you may want to review the section What to STOP Doing Immediately.

9. What is the vibe in our marriage and home? Does our home have a happy, supportive, easygoing, good-humored vibe? Or does it have a negative, critical and cold vibe?

10. Have I been trying, every single day, to put a smile on my spouse's face and make life easier for them? If not, how might that be affecting my spouse or my marriage?

Okay, so there you have it. Ten questions you can ask yourself so that when you talk to your spouse about your problems you already have some insight into what might be going on with them. If you can do that, you'll be able to have a much more purposeful and positive conversation.

For example, if you review question #7—Have I been making my spouse feel appreciated?—and decide that no, you haven't really been putting a lot of effort into that, then that's actually a great insight to know. Now, when you sit down to have a conversation with your spouse, you can admit to that. And that admission just might soften your spouse's heart enough that they will engage in the conversation in a much more collaborative and purposeful way.

Remember—people want to feel heard and understood. If you can do that going into a conversation, you will come out of that conversation much further ahead.

Peace Talks: How to Decode & Understand Your Spouse

You know what decoding is, right? It's the process of translating something, such as symbols or sounds, into an intelligible form. When we think of decoding, we think of something very complicated like the Enigma machine.

If you're not familiar with this, Enigma machines were used by the Nazis in World War II—they were used to encrypt and decrypt secret messages. They allowed German military commanders to send vital instructions pertaining to secret maneuvers and attacks, both on land and at sea. Had the Enigma machine not been decoded by the allies, the outcome of the Second World War might have been very different.

Today, the word *enigma* is used to describe anything that might be a mystery to us, something that's hard to understand or make sense of. Batman's enemy the Riddler is named Edward Nigma…because he's all about solving riddles and figuring things out.

You might feel that way about your partner at times. That you can't figure them out. That they're an enigma. What they're saying, how they're behaving or reacting—it just doesn't make any sense to you.

Worse, it may be that the more you talk about it and try to make sense of it all, the worse things get and the further you get from figuring them out. This happens all the time in relationships and it happens for a number of reasons.

It may happen because your partner simply isn't very good at verbally expressing themselves. Not everyone is. Yet if you are good at verbally expressing yourself, you may assume that your partner should be able to express themselves as easily and insightfully as you can. When something comes naturally to us, we kind of expect that it comes naturally to other people, too.

There's also the fact that some people are very good at putting their foot in their mouth. Regardless of what they're trying to say, even if it's something really positive, it just has a way of coming out all wrong. I'm married to one of these guys, by the way, so you'll forgive me if I express a little more sympathy for these folks. In fact, if you're nodding your head right now and thinking, "That's me!" then hang in there—the next section is for you.

Gender differences can sometimes play into this as well. It's very common for women, who are generally pretty good at verbal expression, to talk circles around men, many of whom aren't as proficient with verbal expression. Yet it certainly isn't always like this. I've worked with many couples where the husband was the stronger communicator of the two. I've also worked with same-sex couples where one partner had great verbal communication skills, but other partner really struggled. So while gender can and often does factor into this, it isn't the only factor.

Another reason why so many couples struggle to communicate is because they tend to try and communicate when emotions—specifically negative emotions—are high, or even at their peak! When we're angry or hurt or fearful or anxious, we can't think straight and we certainly can't articulate our thoughts or feelings very well. We're certainly not in a collaborative spirit, either.

Yet another reason stems from negative experiences. It may be that you or your spouse did express yourselves or communicate well at some point, but were met with defensiveness or criticism or even ridicule.

It may be that in the past you've expressed yourself with all the lyricism of an Italian poet in love, but that—despite the quality of your words—your spouse simply didn't listen or didn't take you seriously. Perhaps nothing changed and so you've just stopped trying.

It may also have something to do with your background, culture or upbringing. Some people are very good at verbally expressing themselves, but they've been raised to think that "men don't talk about their feelings."

At the same time, many people aren't comfortable opening up or talking about their feelings, even if they fully trust their partner to react in a respectful and loving way. They just aren't comfortable talking about themselves in that way or with that kind of depth.

So as you can see, there are many circumstances where a spouse may feel like they have to decode their partner to really figure out what's going on inside.

And that's what we're going to do now. We're going to take a cross-section look at the constituent parts of communication. What does it look like on the inside, so to speak, and how do all of its moving parts work together? We'll decode your spouse so that you can better understand what makes them tick.

Whenever a person says something, there's more to the story that just the words they use. The words are just superficial. There are many things going on under the surface of those words.

Let's look at this context. Imagine a husband is waiting for his wife to get home from work on a Friday afternoon. They had plans to go see a new movie that's opening that night—it's a big sci-fi flick and the husband, who's a huge sci-fi fan, has been looking forward to the movie for months.

Yet his wife is running late and by the time she gets home, it's too late to go and they miss the movie. She walks through the door and is about to apologize, but her husband brushes by her coldly and says, "Save your apology. I'm never going to believe another word you say!" Now, that seems like an immature reaction, and it's definitely not the most sophisticated way to communicate. Saying that he's *never* going to believe another word she says is a little much.

Nonetheless, let's look below the surface of his words, because there's a lot going on.

Perhaps the most obvious thing is **feelings**. A person's emotional feelings definitely influence what they say or don't say.

So this wife has to ask herself: What might my husband be feeling right now? Right off the bat, that's going to give her more insight into him and how he's communicating. In this case, I think it's safe to say that he's feeling anger and disappointment, both toward her and because he was really looking forward to the movie. We can all identify with looking forward to something and then being disappointed when it didn't happen.

Yet too often, we focus only on feelings when we're trying to figure each other out. Think of the marriage counselor who keeps asking, "Tell me how that made you feel?" We do that as partners, too. We ask, "Why do you feel that way?" and maybe even say, "Well, you shouldn't feel that way." That's okay to some extent. It's important to talk about feelings and even challenge them at times, but there's more to it. Human beings and communication are complicated things. There's more going on under the surface than *just* feelings.

Like what, you ask? Well, for starters, there's our own **personality traits.**

I talked about that extensively in part one. That's because, in my opinion, our personality traits and behaviors, our habits, greatly determine the quality of our relationships and the way we communicate.

In the case we're looking at, the wife would be wise to think about that and take her husband's personality into account. It may be that he's a bit of a reactive personality type—he's quick to anger, but he's just as quick to come down and put things in perspective.

So already we have two things that influence the way we communicate, including what we say and how we say it: our feelings and our unique personality.

Let's keep going. Another below the surface variable is our **anticipated outcome or expectation**.

What did we anticipate or believe was going to happen in any given situation? Here, it may be that the husband believed his wife would take whatever steps necessary to get out of work early, or at least on time that day. Maybe he planned his whole day around that belief by working extra hard to make sure he was off early that day.

Let's go even deeper to look at the husband's **assumptions**.

It may be that this marriage has been troubled for a while. Perhaps we're dealing with spouses who have a history of doing things like this to each other on purpose, either to hurt or punish each other. So even if the wife didn't intend to be late, it's likely that the husband made the rather unflattering assumption that she did it on purpose.

In fact, assumptions are one of the biggest troublemakers when it comes to communicating and to accurately understanding our spouse, so I just want to stay here for a bit and talk a little more about them.

We all make assumptions, and that can be a problem. Just think about it—what is an assumption? Well, it's something we accept as truth when we don't actually know the truth. Human beings don't like not knowing things. When we don't know something about a person or a situation, we fill in the blanks with our own assumptions. And those assumptions are almost always negative. That's even more so when we're dealing with spouses who already in conflict.

Okay, I know I'm walking you through this decoding exercise using my sci-fi movie couple, but I want to veer off just for a moment to tell you about a case I had years ago, one that has always stuck with me because perhaps more than any other case I've ever had, it illustrates just how destructive assumptions can be. It was a young couple who had only been married about a year, with no kids. They were definitely a couple that had been fighting to get along for quite a while.

They were in the middle of a big heated argument one night about a car they had just bought—it was their first large purchase together, and unfortunately it turned out to be a complete lemon that was forever in the shop. The wife blamed the husband, since he was the one who had insisted they get that particular vehicle.

As the night wore on, their argument grew even hotter and nastier until the wife finally threw up her arms and said something like, "Honestly, I wish that stupid car was here right now instead of in the shop. If it was here, I'd get in and drive to my sister's. I need some air."

When he heard this, the husband made an assumption: he assumed that his wife wanted to get away from him. He assumed his wife wanted to go stay at her sister's. And we can't blame him for that assumption—it's easy enough to interpret what she said in that way. So here's what he did. He called her a taxi and he packed an overnight bag for her.

He didn't do this belligerently. In fact, quite the opposite. He thought he was being helpful. His wife had stated before that she sometimes wanted space and to stay at her sister's when they were arguing, so he assumed that's what she wanted and that she'd actually be touched by his gesture of calling her a taxi and packing her bag. To him, it was a way of saying, "I respect your space and I'll do whatever it takes to make you happy."

But his wife took it very differently. She made the assumption that he couldn't wait to get rid of her! She was deeply hurt.

So she ripped the bag out of his hands, told him the marriage was over, and stormed out of the house and into the taxi. Of course, he was totally baffled. Didn't he just do exactly what she wanted? Why did it make things worse?

I started working with this couple about six months after this event. They had been separated since that night, but had decided to come to couples' mediation to see whether the marriage could be saved. It was a good thing, too, since it was during the very first consult with each of them that I discovered the way their respective assumptions had absolutely decimated their relationship that night.

That discovery was an incredibly emotional realization for both of them—the realization that their own assumptions had so seriously and so horribly misled them and caused so much heartache. It wasn't a lack of love that had brought them to the brink of divorce. It was a lack of understanding, and their assumptions were to blame for that.

When I was able to look back on that event with them, it all made sense. When we cut out those assumptions and instead figured out what was really going on with each of them in that moment, the fog and confusion cleared. The husband was able to realize that the wife didn't want to leave—what she actually wanted in that moment was for him to put his arms around her and say, "I need some air, too. Let's stop this and go for a walk together. Because I love you and this argument is getting out of control."

At the same time, the wife realized that her husband didn't want her to go—what he actually wanted in that moment was for her to say, "Come for a walk with me. Because this argument is getting out of hand and we need to cool down. I love you."

Their respective assumptions had also prevented both of them from saying what they really wanted to say. What the husband really wanted to say was this: "Please don't think about leaving. Let's get through this together."

What the wife really want to say was, "I don't want to leave. I want to stay so we can get through this together."

To be fair, this couple had a lot of work to do. They were both very poor communicators and there were a number of other issues going on with them as well. Nonetheless, this case is the poster child for assumptions. It showcases how destructive assumptions can be and how utterly incorrect they can be. It showcases how assumptions can send you down a path that you really don't want to go down.

So remember that. Get your own assumptions under control. And whenever you're trying to figure out what's going on with your partner, whenever you're trying to understand something they say or the way they react to something, ask yourself what assumptions they might be operating under.

Okay, let's get back to my decoding exercise and my sci-fi movie couple. You'll remember the wife was late coming home so they missed the movie the husband had been wanting to see. And you'll remember what he said to her when she did get home: "Save your apology. I'm never going to believe another word you say!"

We've already looked at how his feelings, his personality traits, his anticipated outcome and his assumptions may have factored into this response. So let's keep going and see what else is under the surface. Let's see how else we can decode a spouse.

The next under-the-surface component is **fear and/or worst-case-scenario thoughts**.

Fear is a huge one. And guess what? Those assumptions I just talked about are often grounded in our fears—specifically, our worst fears. Here, the husband's worst fear was that his wife didn't love him anymore. After all, she couldn't even be bothered to remember the movie night that they'd had planned for weeks. That must mean she'd given up. That must mean she'd emotionally checked out of the marriage.

Fear is like a ghost: present, but shrouded, and difficult to see or feel. Fear is often shrouded in another emotion, such as anger. Much behavior that looks like raw, simple anger is in reality fear-based.

This is important to realize, since a spouse is often more sympathetic toward a partner's feelings of fear than toward their expressions of anger. Plus, it often happens that both partners are feeling fear, whether for the same or different reasons.

When it comes to understanding and communicating with your spouse, you need to know their fears. Are they afraid you don't love them? Are they afraid of debt? Are they afraid you cannot be trusted or relied upon? Are they afraid you'll never change or aren't motivated enough to change? Are they afraid they don't know how to talk to you or explain themselves? What is their worst fear or the worst-case scenario they've ever shared with you?

Fear underlies a lot of our interactions and reactions, and it factors into so much of our communication. So always ask yourself: What might my spouse be afraid of?

Moving on, we have a person's **worldview**. A person's worldview is just that—the way they view the world. It's their philosophy and their point of view on things. It's their general outlook and attitude toward life.

It encapsulates their ethical or moral principles, and their spirituality. They may be a religious person or an atheist, but regardless, their worldview will affect how they assess, interact and communicate with other people, including their spouse, and how they respond to conflict.

A person's worldview also includes their political opinions. This is an issue that, more and more, seems to be seeping into marriages and other interpersonal relationships to create problems. When I first began my practice, this was rarely if ever a point of contention between spouses; now, I see it all the time.

This is another big one: **unfulfilled needs**. Much conflict, poor behavior and miscommunication is driven by a person's unfulfilled needs. That is, what do they need or want that they're not getting?

In this case, the husband has an unfulfilled need for reassurance. He needs to be reassured that his wife loves him and is committed to him and the marriage. He needs to be reassured that she's willing to put some effort into spending time with him and remembering things that are important to him. Yet her behavior isn't reassuring, and that sparks a really negative reaction from him.

In a lot of cases, people aren't fighting about something that has happened—rather, they're fighting about something that hasn't happened. They're fighting about a need that hasn't been filled. They're fighting or arguing or having problems because of something they're not getting from the relationship. There's a void of some kind, and it's making them unhappy or uneasy.

Aristotle said, "Nature abhors a vacuum." By that, he meant that unfilled spaces are unnatural and contradict the laws of nature. It's the same way in marriage! An unfilled space—a gaping human need of some kind—isn't natural. It needs to be filled, and unless and until it is, there cannot be a natural state of harmony.

There are any number of needs in a marriage, and when they go neglected or unfulfilled, trouble surfaces. However, there are a handful of core needs that I'd like to single out here.

These are: the need to be appreciated, the need to be heard, the need to be validated, the need to be reassured, the need to be prioritized, the need to be respected, and the need to feel loved.

In fact, we can see that this husband has a few unfulfilled needs in the marriage—the need to be reassured of his wife's love, the need to be respected, and the need to be prioritized. And that's not a good thing. The more gaping needs a person has in their marriage, the more they're going to be unhappy and dissatisfied with that marriage.

So the next time you need to decode your spouse or something they say or do, ask yourself: What is my partner's unfulfilled need right now? What do they need that they're not getting from me? What void needs to be filled before we can have some harmony, here? That's a good place to start.

Another variable to consider when decoding your partner's words or behavior is the **impact or consequences** that your behavior, or the conflict, has had on their life in a practical sense.

That's something that too few people give any thought to whatsoever, to perfectly honest. In the case of our sci-fi movie couple, it's possible that the wife either didn't want or wasn't willing to make any changes to her workday to accommodate her husband's desire to see the movie. She may have seen that as an inconvenience that she wasn't willing to accept. All she could see was how the situation affected her.

And unfortunately, that's what many people are like. They are very self-focused and quickly come to resent any requests or accommodations asked of them. At the same time, they often don't give a second thought to the impact or consequences that their own behavior or the conflict has on their partner!

Here's what I mean by this. In our sci-fi scenario, it may be that this husband had arranged for a babysitter for the kids. Maybe he had already packed up all the kids and driven across town to pick up the babysitter and bring her back, and maybe they had all been waiting at the house for hours for the wife to get home so they could leave for the movie. Maybe he had made reservations at a restaurant for after the movie, which he had intended to be a sweet surprise for his wife.

Maybe he now had to drive the babysitter back across town and pay her for her time, cancel the reservations, and all for nothing. It may be that the wife's failure to come home early, which she had said she was going to do, cost him a lot in terms of his time, effort, money—and emotion.

So always think about this. Because a lot of people don't, and it causes a lot of hard feelings and nasty reactions.

Ask yourself: What impact has this had on my spouse in a practical sense? Has it been an inconvenience for them? Has it cost them time, energy or effort? Has it been emotional for them?

Here is the next variable to consider in our cross-section / decoding exercise: **hopes and dreams.** It isn't just bad things that factor into our reactions and communication. In my experience, most couples who are fighting to get along are truly and deeply in love with each other. They have great hopes and dreams for their marriage and their family. They have beautiful hopes and dreams for their future as a couple. Melt-your-heart kind of hopes and dreams. Yet when they're not communicating or understanding each other, those hopes and dreams get blown away in the wind.

In the case of our sci-fi movie couple, the husband may have had all kinds of hopes for his marriage. He may have hoped that they had turned a corner and that this sort of behavior—forgetting or not prioritizing things that were important to the other person—was behind them. He may have dreamed of better days ahead. And when he was disappointed yet again by his wife, it felt to him like all that hope and all those dreams just dissolved into thin air.

Another good thing that often factors into our behavior, even though it may not look like a good thing at the time, is our **intentions**. Most spouses have very good intentions. They want to do the right thing, but unfortunately, their intentions go sideways or are misunderstood.

In this case, the husband's intention was noble: he was trying to set up a fun date night for him and his wife. Yes, he was the one who wanted to see the sci-fi movie, but he had made a reservation at his wife's favorite restaurant for after the movie. He had even asked for the table at the back, by the window, the one he knew she liked best. Yet sadly, that intention never made it to the wife. She may have assumed his intention was just to see the movie he wanted, and to drag her along with him even though she isn't a huge sci-fi fan.

I'll often find myself speaking with an angry spouse, someone who's complaining about something their spouse did, and I'll stop them mid-sentence to ask, "Was that your spouse's intention? Was their intention to make you mad or hurt you or inconvenience you?"

And guess what? The answer is almost always no.

So ask yourself that question: What was my partner's true intention in all of this?

Unfortunately, we often assume that our partner's intentions are bad. We assume that they are intentionally trying to hurt us or anger us or disrespect us. Yet at the same time, we dismiss or justify our own bad behavior. We say, "Oh, I didn't mean to do that" or "I had no choice but to do that" or "My partner misinterpreted what I did."

So just remember that. If your behavior wasn't intentionally bad, it's unlikely your partner's behavior was intentionally bad. Cut them the same slack you cut yourself.

Another variable is **past experiences or issues**.

Whenever spouse communicate, and especially when they're communicating about emotional issues, their respective past experiences may influence the way they interpret and respond to each other's words and actions.

In this case, we've already established that this marriage has a history of both spouses letting each other down, often deliberately so, to hurt or to punish each other. So that's certainly factoring into the husband's reaction. He's been here before and he's sick and tired of it.

But past issues may extend back further, into one's previous relationships or even into childhood.

It may be that this husband saw his mother treat his father the same way: forgetting things, dismissing things that were important to his father, and so on. So in a way, he's supersensitive to that. But he also recognizes the behavior and he doesn't want to live like that.

Similarly, if a person was in a previous intimate relationship with someone who cheated on them, they may become unduly suspicious if their current spouse deletes the text message history on their phone. Their spouse might only be cleaning up their phone, but to their partner, the behavior looks secretive and guilty.

Remember, once bitten, twice shy. So ask yourself: Is there anything in your past history as a couple, or in your partner's past history in a larger sense, that might be factoring into their behavior or the way they are communicating with you?

All right, we're getting to the end here. One of the last factors I want to mention is **personal bias or prejudice**. You know what this is—it's when a person shows support for, or resistance to, something or someone in a way that is unfair, and that is based on their personal opinion.

You might think this only causes problems when it involves major biases or prejudices such as racism or sexism. You'd be wrong. I once really struggled to help a couple where the husband had a strong bias against pit-bull dogs. The wife was involved in a pit-bull rescue and loved the breed, while he felt they should be banned and euthanized en masse. They ended up divorcing. Obviously, there was more to it than this, there were all kinds of assumptions going on, and their personality traits and worldviews were certainly factoring into their problems as well. Nonetheless, I'm sure you can see how this contributed to the marriage's demise.

Finally, the last of the variables I want to mention in this decoding exercise is **self-image**. How does your partner see themselves? By extension, do they have healthy self-perception and good self-esteem? And perhaps more specifically, how are your marriage problems affecting the way they see or feel about themselves? Many people who are struggling in their marriages feel a sense of failure or even a loss of dignity or identity.

In this case, the husband may be struggling with a loss of dignity as he ponders how many times his wife has disrespected him, but how he's always forgiven her. This hurts his self-perception, and he brings that pain into the way he communicates with her.

I see this quite a bit when I'm dealing with infidelity situations. I've dealt with many betrayed spouses who were willing to work through their partner's infidelity; however, they really struggled with their self-perception and self-esteem.

A betrayed wife might say, "I feel like I'm being weak and stupid if I take him back. I don't want to be that person." At the same time, a betrayed husband might say, "I'll always be the guy whose wife cheated on him."

So ask yourself: "How might our marriage problems, or my own behavior, be affecting my spouse's self-image? Might it be taking a toll on their self-perception, self-esteem, or self-worth?"

Yet a person's self-image and sense of self-worth can swing to the other extreme, too. It can be too grandiose. Some people have a streak of egotism or even narcissism in them. They perceive themselves as being superior to other people and that sense of self-importance manifests if a number of ways, each more unappealing than the last. We'll look at this more closely in part three of this book, because self-importance is definitely one of the more difficult and obnoxious behaviors to deal with.

So as you can see, there is a lot more to communication than what someone says or doesn't say. There are a lot of things going on under the surface, a lot of things that their words don't reveal.

In the case we've been following, the husband's initial reaction did at first come across as a simple overreaction: "Save your apology. I'm never going to believe another word you say!" It sounded almost childish. Yet when we look under the surface of those words, we see that there is a lot going on with this man. That awareness makes it possible for us, and his wife if she chooses, to better understand him.

When you're communicating with your partner, especially when you're talking about an emotional issue like a marriage problem, always keep that in mind. Words only sit on the surface. What is below that?

Your partner is dealing with their own feelings, assumptions, fears, worldview, unfulfilled needs, hopes and dreams, biases, and self-image. They aren't just talking or not talking, they're processing the situation in their own way, and on many levels.

When you find yourself struggling to understand your partner, when you wish you could decode their words or behavior, it can be immeasurably helpful to mentally run through these variables and see whether they can give you some insight.

In fact, this decoding exercise does more than just facilitate insight. It also facilitates perspective and empathy and on your part. It may be that you haven't really been thinking about how deeply or diversely your marriage issues have been impacting your partner. Once you go through this exercise and realize how much is going on with your spouse, you may find it easier to see things from their perspective. Fair, but aware, remember? You might also find it easier to have more compassion and patience with them.

Peace Talks: How to Express Yourself Without Starting a War

We've done some work in this part to help you understand your partner and to gain some insight into how your marriage problems may be affecting them on a number of levels. As I said, the more you can understand your spouse, the easier and more effectively you'll be able to communicate as a couple. If you can go into a conversation already having an idea of what your spouse is feeling or thinking or assuming, it's more likely that the conversation is going to be a useful one.

It's important to show your partner that you've been putting a lot of thought into how your marriage problems and your own behavior have affected them. If your spouse can see that you're doing this, it's far more likely they'll return the favor by trying to see things from your perspective.

And that's the spirit we're striving for when we communicate—one where both spouses are truly interested in understanding each other.

So yes, spouses need to understand each other. But they also need to understand themselves.

Here's a common complaint I hear from clients: "I want to know what's upsetting my spouse…I want to figure out why they're unhappy and why we're fighting all the time. But every time I ask them what's wrong or what I can do to make things better, they just say, "I don't know.'"

That response—I don't know—is probably one of those frustrating expressions ever. I mean, just think about it. Let's say you get your phone bill and it's 200% higher than it usually is, although your usage hasn't changed. You call the company and say, "Why is my bill so high?" and the person on the other end of the line says, "I don't know."

Let's say you ask your kid how they did on the math test that was handed back that morning, and they say, "I don't know."

Let's say you ask your family what they want for supper and instead of giving you a suggestion they just say, "I don't know."

It's just a frustrating experience, especially when you're talking to someone who should know, who should be able to contribute something, and who you're relying on to give you the information you need or want.

My point is this: if your partner is trying to get information from you so that they can better understand you and your marriage problems, try not to say, "I don't know." That'll probably just make them frustrated. After all, if you don't know yourself how can they possibly know you?

Plus, saying "I don't know" can come across as indifferent, apathetic and even lazy. It kind of sounds like, "I don't know, and to be honest, I don't care enough to put any thought into it."

Falling back on "I don't know" can also be a control thing: the person who says "I don't know" kind of holds all the power, don't they? They have the information that's needed, but unless and until they choose to share it, things are deadlocked. This leaves the other partner, the one who wants to know the information, in a constant state of uncertainty and speculation.

But pretty soon, that uncertainty and speculation are going to give way to frustration and resentment. Nobody likes to be held hostage. And if you're saying "I don't know," that's basically what you're doing.

For these reasons and others, I want you to steer clear of saying "I don't know." Instead, do a little self-analysis to better understand yourself, so that you can help your partner understand you.

To do this, you might want to use the framework of the decoding exercise in the previous section. You can decode yourself.

Think about the issue or problem that you and your spouse are dealing with at the moment, or something you typically fall into conflict over. And before you have another conversation about it, go through the decoding exercise.

Identify your own feelings and how your personality traits may be factoring into things. Think about your own beliefs, assumptions, worst fears, and worldview. Identify your unfulfilled needs—what are you not getting from the marriage or from your spouse? What are the voids in your marriage or life?

Think about how your marriage problems or your spouse's behavior have impacted your personal or professional life...have there been any negative consequences for you? Identify your hopes and dreams for the marriage. Look at the situation objectively and think about whether your personal biases or past experiences tend to influence the way you think, behave or communicate.

Think about your own self-image, self-perception and self-esteem. How do you see yourself? How do you feel about yourself?

If you've already gone through part one of this book, you've already done some work that involves looking within. That's a good thing. Aristotle—I'll quote him again—said, "Knowing yourself is the beginning of all wisdom." Isn't that the truth. Knowing yourself is also the beginning of being able to express yourself in a meaningful, insightful, collaborative and respectful way.

You and your spouse need to stop having pointless arguments and battles, and you need to have some peace talks. So do the prep work it will take to make sure those peace talks are successful. Try to understand your spouse. Try to understand yourself. Remember that you're allies, not enemies.

Peace Talks: How to Have a Fabulous Conversation About Anything

Let's look at where we are right now. You've shifted the communication dynamics in your marriage so that you're focused on hearing and understanding your partner first. You've gathered intelligence and decoded your spouse to the best of your ability to try and understand them better.

You've even spent some time decoding yourself so that you have more insight into your own side of things, and so that you can express yourself clearly and respectfully to your spouse.

Now it's time to actually have a conversation with your partner. But not just any conversation. Let's aim higher than that. Let's aim to have a fabulous conversation.

Why? Because the more fabulous your conversations are, the fewer of them you'll need to have (at least about issues that are causing conflict). Each conversation has to count. But it has to count *down*. Of course you need to talk about your problems. Of course you need to talk about what's bothering you. Talking is good, but talking about your problems or about what's bothering you can become almost habitual. There comes a point when you aren't talking about it, you're just talking it to death.

The purpose of a heart-to-heart conversation is to move past problems, not wallow in them. If you keep talking about the hurt and resentment, you'll keep reliving the hurt and resentment. You'll start spinning your wheels, digging yourselves further into the muck but getting nowhere, fast. Eventually, you'll start to think that you're stuck for good and that you'll never move forward.

And when couples start to think that way, they begin to lose hope. They start to feel a sense of futility about things, including their future. It destroys those hopes and dreams we talked about. So let's aim for a fabulous conversation, shall we?

Here's an important thing to remember: The best conversations happen when people are at their best and on their best behavior. So before you have any kind of heavy discussion with your partner, I suggest that you finish this book and then flip through the pages again, reminding yourself of key points and also any notes you've made in your scribbler while completing the questions (to all three parts). That'll keep you in the zone by reminding you of those insights and strategies you've found most revealing and useful.

In addition, I'm now going to give you ten overarching communication strategies that should always be front and center in your mind when you need to discuss something serious or possibly incendiary with your spouse. Some of these are mentioned elsewhere, but I wanted to present them here in a more summarizing sort of way.

Please, do not underestimate the value of taking proactive steps to make sure that your conversations remain positive and purposeful! This is a peace talk, remember? Treat it with that level of importance and respect.

1. **Good timing.** A well-timed conversation can do wonders and make things better. A poorly-timed conversation can wreak havoc and make things worse. So put a lot of advance thought into this. When does your spouse seem to be the most receptive to talking?

I'm guessing it isn't the second they walk in the door after work, or in the middle of night when you've woken them from sleep. I'm guessing it isn't after it's taken them two hours to get the kids to sleep.

Don't spring an ill-timed "We need to talk" conversation on your spouse. To increase your chances of a successful conversation, you can schedule a time and be sure you've limited distractions (the kid are sleeping or at grandma's, your phones are turned off, the cat's out, that kind of thing). A spontaneous conversation can work too, especially if you and your spouse are in a particularly open-minded, collaborative mindset and mood.

Also, keep an eye on the clock. Heavy conversations shouldn't drag on…and on….and on…. Be sure to stay tuned-in to the mood, and if it starts to deteriorate, end the conversation in a respectful way, perhaps indicating when you'll pick it up again so you aren't left feeling that issues are unresolved.

2. **A good environment.** Try not to have this fabulous conversation in the same area that you and your partner tend to fight in. That is, if you tend to argue in bed or while sitting on the couch, don't choose those spots for your peace talks! Where should you go? I don't know. Sit in the bath together. Go have a romantic dinner out and talk. Go stay in a hotel and talk. Go take an evening stroll together and talk as you walk under the stars, or take an evening drive and grab a couple milkshakes and a basket of onion rings as you talk it out. Shake it up and let the fabulous happen.

3. **A good mood.** Talking by candlelight, playing soft music or even having a funny movie playing in the background can all help create a good mood or atmosphere. Of course, playing *The Three Amigos* while talking about a spouse's affair isn't going to be appropriate; however, it might set the perfect mood if you're talking about something less painful. Use your discretion and common sense, as well as your knowledge of your spouse.

Just remember that the point isn't to trivialize what you're talking about, but to balance a heavy conversation with a lighter mood so the discussion doesn't descend into a bitter argument.

4. **A good attitude.** Yes, you and your spouse may have some bad feelings toward each other right now; however, you should try to balance those negative feelings with more positive ones—that starts with having good thoughts. Stay in a positive frame of mind by reminding yourself of the good things your spouse has done for you, your friends or family, or of how they've contributed to your life or home. When we're angry with someone, it's all too easy to forget that person's better qualities and the many ways they've been loving to us in the past.

5. **Keep it coming.** As you and your spouse talk through your problems, you will hear things you don't like and that you may disagree with. You may feel hurt or offended. Keep this in mind: As long as your spouse is being honest, fair, and respectful of your feelings, they're entitled to express their legitimate complaints about the marriage.

In fact, you want them to express themselves. You want your spouse to keep talking. You don't want them to shut-down and stop talking. You want to make progress. To do that, you'll need to hear them out. So instead of punishing your spouse for what they say and shutting them down, encourage them to keep talking. After all, you'll undoubtedly be saying things that they may find hurtful too, right? So lead the way. Show them that both of you have the freedom to say what you need to say.

6. **Watch your tone!** Please, I beg you, keep your ears open during peace talks to ensure that your voice tone doesn't take on shades of defensiveness, sarcasm, criticism, derision or impatience. These are not pacifying tones—they're war cries. Keep your voice tone respectful, even affectionate, at all times. Don't adopt a fake tone, but don't adopt an awful one, either.

7. **Watch your tongue!** Trust me, I'm no prude when it comes to the more colorful words in the English language. Nonetheless, I strongly advise against using profanity or other very strong, potentially off-putting language during peace talks. It just isn't the right time or place. Bringing harsh words into what should be a peaceable conversation is just too risky. Hold yourself and your word choice to a higher standard during this very important conversation. After it's over, when you're looking back at how useful the conversation was from a distance, you can congratulate each other on how fucking fabulous it was.

8. **Control your *extremes* of emotion.** It is normal, healthy, and expected to show emotion during any conversation. That's what we do as humans and it's an essential part of communication. We rely on reading facial expressions, body language, and interpreting voice tone. We can "read" the emotions coming off another person, and that helps us understand how they are interpreting what we say or what effect our message is having on them. That's one way we learn about each other.

That process is important, so don't ever think that you need to shut down your emotions or responses during a conversation. That would be impossible, unfair and counter-productive to our purpose. A couple should be able to continue a fabulous conversation even through passing periods of reasonable and controlled anger, sadness, or other emotion.

Problems arise when the emotions become unreasonable and uncontrolled. That might be an outburst of anger or accusation. Or it might be total emotional withdrawal—that's a type of extreme, too, isn't it? In these cases, spouses are unable to continue with the conversation because the extreme display of emotion has just been too jarring and too distracting. Instead of enhancing our message, the extreme emotion obliterates our message.

As bad, when one or both spouses show extremes of emotion—at least on a regular basis—during conversation, it's only a matter of time until one or both spouses refuse to engage in conversation in the future.

So by all means, show emotion. You have a right to your emotions, and so does your partner. Respect yours and respect theirs. But don't let *extremes* of emotion sabotage your peace talks.

9. **Don't interrupt.** A lot of what I've said here and elsewhere in the book really boils down to having good "marriage manners." But a fabulous conversation requires its own set of manners, and perhaps one of the biggest is to not interrupt your spouse any more than is absolutely necessary.

Few things make a person feel less heard and more irritated during a conversation than being interrupted. You may occasionally need to interrupt your partner to ask something or to clarify something they said; however, just be sure that you aren't interrupting them to defend yourself, contradict something they said, or offer unnecessary feedback.

Remember that built-in "let me go first" setting we all have? Try to temporarily deactivate yours, and let your spouse get it all out.

10. **Realize this isn't an urgent situation.** Humans are impatient creatures. When we want something done, we want it done right now. We want our spouse to understand us and agree to make changes, and we want them to do that "right now." We want our marriage problems to be over "right now," too. I want your marriage problems to be over too, and I want that to happen as quickly as possible. In fact, every insight and strategy I suggest in this book is geared toward ending conflict and improving your marriage in the shortest time possible. I know you want to get on with life. With a happier life.

But that's not going to happen in the course of one conversation. Things may start to improve, maybe even significantly, but it's unlikely that one conversation is going to fix all your problems. So don't approach it with that sense of urgency or finality. Don't put that much pressure on it! If you do, you're only setting yourself up for disappointment and frustration, and all for no reason. This is not an urgent situation. Slow down, talk through it, get through it, day by day.

These ten communication tips are things I want you to consider whenever you and your spouse have a heavy type of conversation. If you can keep things like timing, environment and voice tone in mind, you'll stand a much better chance of your peace talks actually achieving their goal.

Peace Talks:
The Secret Weapons of Fabulous Communication

In my ongoing pursuit to show you and your spouse how to have the most fabulous conversation ever, I want to go through a few more strategies you can implement. I know you may be dealing with some heated issues, so the more tools I can give you to cool things down, the better.

The first secret weapon strategy is called **the sandwich method** and the name says it all. It involves sandwiching a negative or perhaps touchy message between two positive messages. You start by saying something nice, then you get to the meaty not-so-nice middle part, and then you end with something nice.

Let's see it in action. Let's say it's a second marriage situation for a certain man. He has a twelve year old son, called Carter, from his first marriage, and every second weekend, Carter comes to stay with him, his new wife and the nine-year-old son they have together.

Yet the husband has noticed how his wife seems to be treating Carter quite poorly. She is fairly impatient with him and is starting to snap at him more and more. If she runs to the store, she comes home with a surprise or treat for her child, but nothing for him.

If this man didn't know the sandwich method, he might say something like: "You know, it seems like you're turning into the typical evil stepmother. I mean, how petty can you be? You bring our kid candy but nothing for Carter? Nice. Maybe try not being such a bitch to a twelve-year-old kid."

Yeah, that's probably not going to make life better for anyone, including Carter. He's no closer to getting candy from his stepmom, that's for sure.

Now let's serve up this message using the sandwich method.

First part, fairly pleasant: "Sweetheart, I love you and I can't thank you enough for welcoming Carter into our home. I know he's at that tough age, and that his visits do affect our plans."

Middle part, not as pleasant: "Yet lately it seems like Carter is treated differently when he's here than our son is, and I'm worried that's going to affect the way he feels about both of us, and his stepbrother. I want them to be close, for both their sakes. I'd really appreciate it if you would just be extra aware of that so it doesn't happen."

Third part, back to pleasant: "Thank you for listening. I knew I married the right woman this time."

Of course I'm oversimplifying here. Stepfamily situations are incredibly complicated. Nonetheless, you can see how this general approach is more purposeful and respectful than just getting mad, making assumptions or accusations, and throwing insults that only widen the divide between everyone involved.

This approach is also more likely to spark a useful and mature conversation in this marriage and perhaps even the larger household, as the wife feels appreciated rather than maligned.

So remember the sandwich method if you have to broach a touchy subject with your spouse: start with something loving and flattering, say what you have to say in the middle, and then end with something loving and positive.

The second secret weapon strategy is called **reframing.** I like to think of this as taking an ugly picture and putting an attractive frame around it, so that whole thing looks like art. In the context of communication, reframing is when we present a fairly unappealing message in a very appealing way.

Imagine a wife is frustrated with the lack of time and attention her husband has been showing their three young kids. It seems like he'd rather do anything other than be with his kids.

Here's how she might talk to her husband about it if she'd never heard of reframing. She might throw up her arms in frustration and shout, "Honestly, I might as well be a single mom! You live in the same house as your kids, but you're a deadbeat dad. They barely know who you are. If you don't want to be here, then go, get out!"

Now, let's reframe that message. First, instead of throwing up her arms and shouting, this wife brings her husband a cup of coffee and sits next to him on the couch. "Chris," she says, "did I tell you how much the kids loved it last weekend when you took them to the park? They talked about it for days. I know you have a lot on the go, but I think it would be great if you could do that more often. I worry they aren't getting the daddy time they need. And they do need it. Whenever they spend time with you, they just seem to behave so much better and seem much happier. They're so lucky to have you as their dad."

Does this strike you as sappy? It better not, because this is what a father wants to hear. And if this wife wants her husband to feel invested in their family life, she has to reframe that message—you need to spend more time with your kids!—in a way that her husband will respond to in a positive way. And the frame she's put around this is one that makes him feel needed as dad. That's going to motivate him a lot more than calling him a deadbeat dad.

Let's look at another example. Take the case of a husband who's getting really frustrated at the lack of sex in his marriage. Here's how he might broach this subject with his lovely wife if he'd never heard of reframing.

He might sigh heavily, throw up his arms, and say, "For god's sake, I didn't get married to live like a monk. It's always an excuse with you, isn't it? *I don't feel well, the kids are sick, I'm too tired...*blah blah. It's always something."

Yeah. I don't think this is going to improve this man's chances. Let's see if reframing can have better luck.

He might try to say something along these lines: "Sweetheart, I know you have going on in your life, probably a lot more than I'm aware of it, but I want to talk to you about something. It feels like we're losing some of that passion we used to have and that scares me. I miss you. I miss having fun with you and being close to you in that way. Is there something I'm doing that's preventing that from happening? Is there something I can help you with so you aren't always so tired? You're a great mom and you do your best, but those kids are exhausting."

So that's reframing. It's an incredibly versatile and useful strategy, so keep it in mind. Almost any picture can look a little better with a good frame around it. It just takes a little thought.

Moving on, the third secret weapon is to **give your spouse the spotlight**. Most people like to talk about themselves. They like to talk about their experiences and emotions and memories and insights, and they especially like to talk about these things with people who are important to them. That's okay. Every now and then it's perfectly fine to want that spotlight.

Picture this. A wife comes home after a long, hard, frustrating day at the office. She sits down next to her husband and says, "I had a crazy day at work. You know that idiot Karen? Well, you won't believe what she did."

The husband chuckles and says, "I promise, as crazy as your day was, mine was crazier. Never mind Karen, you won't believe what Jim did. Let me tell you…" and then he goes on to tell her. And in the process, he's stolen her spotlight.

We all do this from time to time. Maybe what Jim did was more idiotic than what Karen did, and so the wife won't mind hearing about it; however, if a couple isn't getting along that well, this habit can come across as dismissive and can become quite irritating.

Imagine that a couple is driving in their car on their way to a weekend getaway. Their marriage has been strained lately with lots of bickering back and forth, and generally a lot of negativity. They're hoping to reconnect. An old song comes on the radio and the wife says, "Oh man, I used to love this group. I saw them in Seattle when I was in university. What a great time that was."

The husband says "I never liked them." He takes a sip of his coffee and asks, "How far back was that gas station we filled up at? I want to figure out what kind of gas mileage this car gets. I guy I work with is thinking of buying one and I told him I'd keep an eye on it."

Do you see what happened here? The wife was enjoying a bit of nostalgia and was basically inviting her husband to ask her more about it. She wanted to talk about herself a bit—that's not always a bad thing. She wanted to share a memory and an important time of her life with her husband.

But he didn't pick up on the cue. Instead, he just kind of shouldered his way into her spotlight and took it over by talking about a completely unrelated issue—gas mileage.

So look for those cues. Look for those times when your spouse wants to stand in the spotlight for a while, whether it's to relive a memory, share a problem, or even express a concern about the marriage. If they start talking, let them. Make it all about them for a while.

Don't try to one-up their story, don't try to solve their problems, and definitely don't jump in and start telling them why they're wrong or why they shouldn't feel that way. Don't jump in and defend yourself or start sharing anecdotes of your own without even commenting on theirs.

Instead, show your spouse that you're a captivated audience. Show them you're curious about what they have to say. You care. You're interested and you're willing to spare some of your time to listen to them talk and to let them have the spotlight.

You can learn a lot about your spouse this way. You can also be certain that when it comes time for you to want the spotlight and talk, they'll actually listen. So lead the way.

The fourth secret weapon is to **lighten up**. Now, there are definitely times it's appropriate and necessary to approach problems with gravity. But it isn't always necessary. A lot of the time, we approach communication or conflict in a negative way when we just don't have to. And if this becomes a habit or our default way of expressing ourselves, the people around us are going to start shutting down and resenting us.

Take the case of a wife and mom who's ready to pull her hair out because every morning the kitchen turns into a disaster zone as her husband and kids scramble to make their breakfast and lunches. Typically, she might say, "You guys are a bunch of slobs! You leave jam all over the counter, you spill cereal everywhere, you don't put anything back in the fridge…I'm so sick of being the one who has to clean up everyone else's mess!"

This might be true—it probably *is* true—but it's likely that this approach is only going to make mom come across as short-tempered and everybody's going to start getting defensive.

Here's another way to handle it: Mom might come in and say, "You guys, our poor kitchen looks like a tornado goes through it every morning at seven o'clock. I'd like to institute project clean counter. Let's have mercy on our kitchen, okay? And on your poor mom who has to sweep up the aftermath every morning."

By taking this approach, she's still getting her message across—*Hey, I'm the one who has to clean all of this up every morning and I'm getting tired of it*—but she's delivered that message in a lighter way, in a way that is more likely to be heard. It's more likely to create a sense of solidarity and to make her husband and kids look at their own behavior and clue in to the fact that poor mom is left with a mess every morning. It's more likely to inspire them and make them want to help mom instead of roll their eyes at her outburst.

Plus, instead of nagging every morning, all these parents have to do now is simply say the words "project clean counter" to their kids to remind them to clean up after themselves. This light-hearted prompt is certainly better than mom having to nag them about it every morning, which drives everyone crazy.

Now, this clean-counter example also showcases the fifth secret weapon strategy, which is to **depersonalize your problems**. You'll notice that this mom didn't point fingers—she didn't say "You're doing this, you're doing that!" Instead, she focused on the problem—the messy kitchen. She focused on the problem and not the person. By doing this, she limited the chance that her husband or kids would get defensive. After all, she wasn't singling anyone out. She was just identifying a problem that affected the home and therefore the whole family. It wasn't personal.

That's something you should try to do as much as possible. Focus on the dynamics or the interactions or the problem rather than the person. It isn't always possible or appropriate to do this—sometimes we do have to call someone on their behavior—but we don't always have to communicate or approach conflict that way. Depersonalize your problems whenever you can. You'll sidestep a lot of defensiveness, hard feelings and finger-pointing.

The sixth secret weapon is to **ask for and accept input**. Sounds simple, right? You'd think so. But most of us don't do it.

Here's the case that springs to my mind. A couple had been struggling with the bedtime routines of their two kids. The mom was a stay-at-home mom, but the dad didn't get home in the evenings until after seven o'clock. Since the kids went to bed at eight o'clock, he didn't get to see them for very long. Anyway, the wife had joined a gym—two or three nights a week she'd leave as soon as her husband got home from work, so it was his responsibility to put the kids to bed.

When I spoke to this wife, here's what she said: "I'm so frustrated and mad at my husband, I can't even tell you how mad I am. He came home on Friday at seven-thirty and I told him the kids had to go to bed at eight. That's what we agreed on. But when I came home at nine, the kids were still up. He was sitting in the backyard having a drink with the neighbor, and the kids were running around like a bunch of wild animals."

"Really?" I asked. "Like wild animals? Like loose running up and down the street?"

"No, they were in the backyard with him, but they were wired. And it was past their bedtime. I was mad, because we agreed on that bedtime, so I grabbed the kids and took them in and then guess what? Then he comes into the house and he's mad at me!"

"I can't blame him," I said. "The poor man's trying to enjoy a nice drink in the backyard with his neighbor on a Friday night, he's having a nice time watching his kids play, and then you come home and crash the party."

Obviously this isn't what my client was expecting to hear, so she persisted. "We both agreed the kids would be in bed at eight o'clock. He shouldn't have agreed to it if he wasn't going to do it."

"Did you really both agree?" I asked her, "or did you say that's the way it was going to be, and that was the agreement?"

"We talked about it," she said, "and he had his chance to say his bit."

"Maybe he did," I said. "Is it possible that he disagreed, maybe saying that he wanted to spend more time with his kids in the evening, but you disregarded that and steamrolled ahead with the eight o'clock bedtime? I'm just wondering whether he truly agreed with it, or whether he just gave up and went along with it, because it wasn't worth the fight. And if that was the case, it wouldn't be an agreement. Nonetheless, now you get to take the high ground by saying he agreed to it, so it's all his fault. Tell me honestly—am I right about any of this or am I completely missing the mark?"

This woman was totally silent for about ten seconds. Then she said, "That's exactly what happened. He didn't want to agree to it, but yeah, I steamrolled him."

"Great," I said. "Now we know. Now you know. Now go back and apologize for crashing the party. Go back and apologize for embarrassing him in front of the neighbor, and instead tell him how wonderful it is that he wants to spend more time with his kids. And then go back to the drawing board with bedtimes. This time, actually ask for his input and accept it."

And that's what I want you to do, too. Whenever you're talking to your partner about something, and especially when you're trying to make plans or resolve your problems, always ask for your spouse's input. And then accept it.

This doesn't mean you're letting them decide on the final outcome—it just means that you're working collaboratively and that both of you are able to offer ideas, input, that is equally respected and considered. A marriage is a partnership, not a dictatorship.

The seventh secret weapon is to **know your audience**. I do a lot of radio, everything from very high-brow talk radio to morning radio on top-forty stations. Those are very different audiences, and I know that going in. I know my audience. I know when I can tell an off-color joke or come across as irreverent, and I know when I need to keep it more scholarly and refined.

So let me ask you: do you know your audience? I mean, I know you know them—you're married to them—but have you really stopped to think about how they tend to receive messages? Have you really stopped to consider their sensibilities and personality, and how you can best get your message across to them?

It's popular nowadays for people to classify or categorize their partner as this type of spouse or that. Personally, I don't like that approach. For me at least, it's too rigid. People change, by the minute sometimes, depending on their mood, assumptions, or anticipated outcomes. I think it's better to simply study your audience and to know them as an individual.

Put some thought into this. When does your spouse seem most receptive to talking? When does your spouse seem to join in conversation? Are you driving in the car or walking hand in hand? Are you sitting on the couch playing video games or are you eating supper? Do they seem most willing to talk in the morning over coffee or do they like pillow talk?

Also, what actions on your part tend to get your spouse to relax and open up? What kind of voice tone or attitude do they respond positively to? In a larger sense, what tends to make your spouse happy, loving and collaborative?

There's no substitute for tailoring your communication to fit your spouse. It's great to have an arsenal of strategies to choose from, and that's what I'm giving you here, but there's no one-size-fits all when it comes to communication. Know your audience. Better yet, love your audience. Inspire your audience. Do your best to wow your audience and bring them to their feet with applause. That'll get that their attention.

There isn't one communication strategy that is so good, so powerful, that it can open another person's mind and heart. A person has to *want* to do that. It's like anything else—there's no weight-loss strategy, no stop-smoking strategy that will work unless the person really wants to lose weight or stop smoking.

It's not the strategy, it's the person and how motivated they are. It's the overall quality of the marriage and the interactions between partners. It's the overall show, not just any particular scene. So know your audience and play to them.

Keeping the Peace: The Power of Micro Talks

You've probably heard someone talking about how important it is to "keep the channels of communication open" in marriage. Basically, that means staying connected and tuned-in to each other. It means you should be able to talk to each other as problems come up, instead of saving it all up for one big heated argument or all-night talk. That's definitely good advice, but what does it mean in a practical sense? How exactly do you keep the channels of communication open?

Do you just sporadically say, "Hey, if something's bothering you, you can talk to me, you know." Sure. If that's what works for you as a couple, then do it. Do whatever works. As I just finished saying in the previous section, the skill or approach you use isn't as important as knowing your audience and as having a good overall vibe in the marriage.

But if you're looking for a new way to keep the channels of communication open, try having micro talks. Micro talks are brief and positive conversations that target a spouse's specific past complaints (as opposed to being general in nature).

Let's look at one in action. Take the case of a couple that used to argue quite a bit over money. The husband was a chronic spender, but after they had one of their cars repossessed, he changed his ways. Since that time, their marriage has steadily improved.

Nonetheless, he knows that his wife has lingering resentment about the many years he refused to get his spending under control. One day, they're at the beach when he brings his wife and kids ice-cream cones from the snack counter.

He sits next to his wife and says, " Good thing I finally got my act together with the finances, since the prices here are nuts. By the way, how am I doing? I'm trying to stay on track, but make sure you let me know if I'm slipping because I don't want to."

At this point, if there is indeed something that has been nagging at his wife, she has the perfect opening to address it. She knows her husband will listen to her. And if he has been doing a good job of staying on track, there's no harm done—he's simply reinforced the fact that he's taking accountability for his past mistakes, and that he's committed to staying on track. Either way, this informal micro talk has addressed a past conflict in a brief, positive way, and in the process has managed to keep this couple on the same page.

Here's another example. Let's say a certain wife has a long history of being negative and that's caused some problems in the marriage; however, she's been working really hard to have a more positive outlook. One evening, her husband is working on his hobby car in the garage. She brings him a drink and they have some pleasant small talk, and then at some point she says something along the lines of, "I like this. I like when we can just chat like this. It's easier for me now that I'm trying to be more positive. I didn't realize what I was missing. I'm glad you told me how much my behavior was bringing you down."

Now this wife has done a couple things really well, here. She's used good timing, with the husband being relaxed and in a positive mood enjoying his hobby. She's being thoughtful by bringing him a drink and she's acknowledged her past behavior. Plus, by telling him that she's glad he was honest about her behavior, she's sending the message that she's open to receiving any other feedback. So that's all good.

Micro talks can work in the other direction, too. If it's your partner who has been trying to improve their behavior in some way, you can use a micro talk to acknowledge their efforts and to let them know that you appreciate it. This can keep them motivated.

In the case of the couple at the beach, the wife could've brought the tray of food, sat down beside her husband and said, "Food is expensive here. Have I told you how much I love you for what a great job you've done keeping our finances on track? It's hard to break a bad habit, I know, but you're doing wonderfully."

So yes, this idea of keeping the channels of communication open is a good one, but for many people, it's a bit amorphous. They don't know how to do that in a practical sense. If that's you, try a micro talk and see if it works.

To reiterate, micro talks have three characteristics. First, they're brief. Don't start reciting the *Odyssey*—just say your bit and, if your partner doesn't really respond, drop it and move on. Second, micro talks are positive. They focus on the progress you've made and on your commitment to staying on track. Third, they're targeted. They address a specific complaint or issue that you've had in the marriage, one that you and your spouse have been working together to overcome.

Managing Destructive Communication Habits

I want to move on now to talk about how to manage tougher communication problems, the ones that can be particularly destructive to the relationship between spouses.

In part one, we looked at how your personality traits and behaviors factor into the way you interact with your spouse. There's absolutely no doubt that positive interactions between you and spouse provide the very foundation of good communication in a larger sense. It's the dynamics and vibe in the marriage that really determine how well you get along, which in turn affects how well you can talk to each other.

Here in part two, I've covered some great communication strategies. I've talked about how vital it is to hear and understand your spouse, rather than trying to force them to hear and understand you. That's an all-important "you go first" shift to make.

I also talked about the usefulness of doing a little prep work before you just launch into a heavy or emotional conversation. You need to gather some intelligence first so that you can better understand your spouse. There may be elements of their personality, behavior or communication habits that are an enigma to you. That's why I gave you that decoding exercise: there's a lot going under the surface with both you and your spouse.

I then went on to talk about how you could have a fabulous conversation about anything, and also offered some secret weapon strategies of communication.

So as you can see, there's a lot here, and it's all geared toward helping you and your spouse communicate in a positive and purposeful way. But it's also geared toward helping you manage tougher, more destructive communication habits. Because trust me, you're going to need all of these insights and strategies to do that. But it can be done.

Some of the tougher communication habits that I see are defensiveness, finger-pointing or blaming, and the silent treatment. Playing the divorce card is also a fairly prevalent problem: this is when one or both partners threaten divorce as a way to end an argument or conversation. I also see emotional onslaughts, whether those are blow-ups or meltdowns.

I'm going to go through each of these in turn so that you have even more strategies to manage them. Even if you don't struggle with all of these problems, I want you to read through all of them anyway. These habits may present differently, but they often have similar reasons and purposes. That means that solutions that work for one might work for another. In fact, as you'll see, there are some similarities in terms of responding to these. You never know when you'll read an idea that might "click" with you, so be sure to read everything.

But to be honest, the material you've learned to this point is what's really going to help you manage these things if your spouse is doing them. Because quite often, these more difficult communication habits are the result of the way we communicate as a couple. It takes two to tango, as they say.

I've heard many spouses say, "My husband is too defensive," but then once we start looking at the way she talks to him, a lot of that defensive behavior makes sense. It may be that she comes on too strong and instead of admitting to her own shortcomings or trying to hear or understand him, she simply starts blaming him for everything.

Well, anybody would react in a defensive way to that. So you absolutely need to know whether your negative communication habits are prompting your partner to respond with their own negative communication habits.

Yet don't think I'm trying to pin your spouse's destructive communication habits on you! Like you, your spouse is 100% responsible for their own behavior. They are an adult.

I'm simply trying to help you understand whether and how your communication habits might be bouncing off each other. That's a good thing to know, but it does not absolve you or your spouse of your behavior. In the end, both of you are choosing to behave the way you are.

How to Break Through Defensiveness

Okay, let's take a closer look at defensiveness in communication. Take this case. A wife gets home at five o'clock every day and the first thing she does is start supper. She goes to set the table while it's cooking, but there are no clean dishes because her husband—who's the last one out of the house in the morning—forgot to start the dishwasher before he left for work.

When her husband gets home, she says, "You forgot to start the dishwasher this morning and I had to wash everything by hand. Can you please remember tomorrow morning?"

"I didn't forget," he snaps back.

"Well," she says, "you're the last one out of the house and the dishwasher hadn't been turned on."

"Why is it my responsibility to turn on the dishwasher?" he asks. "Can't you do anything around here?"

"I would start the dishwasher but you've told me not to," the wife reminds him. "You said it affects the water pressure when you're having your morning shower, so you promised you'd remember to start it before you leave."

"Then there's something wrong with the dishwasher," he says, "because I wouldn't forget."

"Well, I started it and it's running fine," she says.

"Then what are you complaining about?" he asks. "If it's working, you don't have to wash the dishes by hand. Sounds like you just want to complain."

"The dishwasher cycle takes too long," the wife explains. "So actually I do I have to wash everything by hand or we'd be eating out of the pots."

"There's a pile of paper plates in the cupboard," the husband says. "Instead of whining or trying to blame me, why can't you just handle it and use those?"

Does this exchange sound familiar at all to you? I hope not, because it's an exhausting one. But if it does sound familiar, there are ways to break out of this cycle of defensiveness.

Keep in mind that people tend to behave defensively because they feel attacked—you may not actually be attacking them, but that's how they perceive it.

When the wife opened with, "You forgot to start the dishwasher this morning," her husband immediately felt attacked and criticized.

In a happier relationship, the husband would simply have said, "Oh, whoops, sorry about that. I'll remember tomorrow morning, I promise." He may even have apologized to his wife, realizing that the last thing she wanted to do after work was come home and wash a sink full of dirty dishes!

But not this husband. Instead, it was all about him. He felt he was being attacked—unfairly, of course, so he threw up a defensive wall.

At that point, his wife, whether intentionally or not, began to repeatedly hit that wall by trying to explain herself.

But when you're dealing with a defensive person, that's not going to work. They'll typically see your attempts to explain yourself as continuing attacks against them. The more you try to explain yourself or the situation, the more threatened they feel and the more defensive they get—that's why defensive people often turn loud, belligerent and quite obnoxious. They're trying to get you to back down.

So this begs the question: how could this wife have handled this situation any differently?

Well, one strategy she could have used was to approach the situation indirectly, instead of directly. Let's say she come home and the dishwasher isn't started. Instead of washing the dishes, she could have left them in the dirty dishwasher until her husband came home, as if nothing was up.

As she was busying herself cooking supper, she might have casually said to her husband, "Would you mind setting the table for me? This is going to burn if I don't keep stirring it."

At that point, the husband would have gone to the cupboard, saw there was no dishes, opened the dishwasher and realized he had forgotten to start it. Now, of course he might react in any number of ways. Defensive people can be quite unpleasant. He might have said, "The dishes are all dirty, how do you expect me to set the table?"

At that, the wife—who of course is doing her very best to keep her cool and stay non-reactive—might simply say, "Oh, it must not have been turned on this morning. Would you mind washing up enough plates for supper, please?"

How might the husband respond to this? Who knows. He might do it. He certainly knows he's the one who forgot to start the dishwasher, but how he handles himself at this moment is up to him—it will depend on his character and how motivated he is to keep the peace in his marriage and household.

His wife can only do her part. She can only control her own behavior and the way she speaks to him. She cannot control how he chooses to behave or speak to her. That's on him. And if you're dealing with a defensive spouse, you need to remember that.

Do what you can to speak to your spouse in a way that is non-confrontational and that limits the chances they'll interpret what you say as an attack. Self-check for the ways that your behavior or communication habits may inadvertently be prompting or triggering your partner's negative behavior or communication habits, including their defensiveness. Are you putting out a negative vibe or a positive vibe in the way you speak?

Also, remember that you can't actually "break through" defensiveness. You're a human being, not a battering ram. And by the way, have you ever seen the damage that a battering ram causes? It makes a mess. It's the same thing with defensive behavior. The more you try to break through by meeting your spouse's anger or resistance with your own anger or resistance, the more damage you're going to do.

So despite the heading of this section, don't try to break through defensiveness. Instead, try to find a way around it. Find a place to slip in behind the wall instead of trying to knock it down. That is, try to address the issue indirectly.

You can of course try a more direct approach by talking to your spouse about their defensiveness. Just make sure you keep a few things in mind.

First, make sure you choose the right time. It certainly can't be when your partner is actually being defensive. Second, be sure to admit to your own shortcomings and express a desire to improve those. Third, focus on your feelings instead of your partner's behavior. And fourth, ask for your spouse's input on the matter.

So you might say something like, "I know you have complaints about me, and I'm open to hearing those, but I feel like I can't talk about the things that are bothering me without you shutting down. It makes me sad and worried that we aren't as close as we used to be. Is there anything I can do to make it easier for you to talk to me?"

If your spouse asks for more information—"What do you mean? What are you talking about?"—try to give them an *example* of when you felt that way instead of just saying, "Because you're defensive!"

Perhaps your spouse will listen, and perhaps they won't. If their hackles go up and they start to become defensive even though you're doing your best to keep things non-confrontational and respectful, then stop talking. There's no point beating your head against their wall. Retreat from the battle and go on with life.

Do not allow your partner's behavior to change you or to change the way you live. I don't want you to be passive, but I do want you to avoid those battles you can't win, and which are likely to cause even more damage to your marriage.

The unflattering truth is that some people who exhibit challenging behavior do so for a specific reason—to get their own way. To control a situation, in one way or another, and for one purpose or another. And as I've mentioned before, this can really hurt the healthy balance of power that must exist between spouses.

Yet if your spouse knows that, regardless of how defensive they get, you're still going to do what you're going to do, then the behavior doesn't pay off for them. If they know that, regardless of how defensive they get, you're unmoved by it all, then their behavior just doesn't have the power or effect they're expecting it to have.

That in itself can motivate them to re-examine their own behavior. Frankly, that's what it often takes for a defensive person to lower their guard. So keep that in mind, too. Avoid the payoff. Don't let their behavior pay off or work for them.

Now, I have one more very important thing to mention here about how to manage defensive behavior: I want you to pay close attention to the communications you have with your spouse. If you're talking about something and your spouse does *not* react defensively, or even if they react *less* defensively than usual, I want you to make a big deal of that.

Thank them for it. Tell them how wonderful it was to have a conversation where you felt heard and where you felt the two of you really connected. Show appreciation. Let your spouse know that you know how hard it was for them to lower their guard, and make sure you sing their praises. Flatter them.

Most of us respond better to praise than to criticism. We love to feel appreciated and it feels wonderful to know that someone has acknowledged our efforts or the steps we've taken to do a better job of something.

So show your partner than you admire them. Show them that you admire their strength of character—it's not easy to change, and if they're willing to do it, that's an amazing thing.

Look for an opportunity like that. Even if it's a small one, it's better than nothing. Our goal is for your spouse to realize that an open mind and an open heart feels better than a defensive mind and a defensive heart. So do everything you can to make sure they get to experience that feeling. Many defensive people have never felt it and simply don't know what they're missing!

So if you're dealing with a defensive spouse, be sure to review everything you've already learned so far and keep the most relevant tips in mind (e.g. acknowledge your shortcomings first, listen to their complaints first, let them feel heard and appreciated, ensure you're using the communication strategies you feel would be most helpful, gather intelligence, decode your spouse, etc.).

In addition, keep these most recent anti-defensiveness tips in mind. Try to address the issue indirectly or through a conscious direct conversation, don't reward the behavior (that is, avoid letting it pay off for them), and praise your spouse whenever you see any reduction in their defensive behavior.

How to Stop Pointing Fingers

Let's look now at the blame game. This is when partners get in the habit of pointing fingers and blaming each other for their problems.

"It's your fault!"

"No, it's your fault!"

Let's see what the blame game looks like in full swing.

A husband and a wife are heading to an event—the symphony, a hockey game, the races, it doesn't matter—and as soon as they pull into the car park, the husband says, "Oh no, please tell me you remembered the tickets."

The wife throws up her hands. "No, I asked you to grab them."

"No, you didn't," the husband says. "They were on your desk. How could you forget them?"

"I didn't forget them. You forgot them!"

And so on and so forth, until they're either screaming at each other or giving each other the cold shoulder for the whole ride home.

Here, both partners are playing the blame game. But often, just one is doing it, and it often involves a lot more serious issues than a pair of forgotten tickets.

I've seen wives blame their husbands for the fact that they had to put their career on hold while their kids were young, even though the decision to have kids and for the wife to stay at home was a mutual one.

I've seen husbands blame their wives for the financial debt they're in, even though the husband was one who repeatedly made large impulse purchases they couldn't afford.

I've seen people blame their spouse for their own infidelity. "You weren't having sex with me, so I had to get it somewhere." Or "You never talk to me so I had to find someone who would."

The circumstances can be almost anything. That's because it isn't about the circumstances. It's about the person and what's going on with them.

If you recognize this in the way you and your spouse communicate, then as always, I want you to start with yourself, first. Is it possible that your partner and you have fallen into the blame game and you're more of a participant than you thought?

This dynamic often develops in longer-term relationships. When we're first together, we don't typically blame our partner for things. If anything, we apologize and take on the blame even when we're not at fault! That's because we are more concerned with preserving the relationship than with pointing fingers or figuring out who was at fault.

That changes as times goes on. And that's because we change. Our interactions and the way we feel and communicate change, too. We're focused less on the big picture—"Hey, let's have a good time together"—and more on the little details. "No, *you* forgot the tickets!"

Sometimes, a partner will start pointing fingers out of frustration. They may have a legitimate complaint or concern that they've tried to express in the past, but perhaps their spouse didn't listen. It may be that they simply didn't know how else to handle the situation, so they just started blaming their partner for things.

Other times, a partner will place blame with their spouse as a way to avoid taking responsibility for their own behavior or to avoid admitting something they've done wrong.

It may be that they're afraid to admit it. Perhaps their spouse isn't a forgiving soul or overreacts when they do admit to doing something wrong.

Yet as often as not, finger-pointing is exactly what it looks like—someone who is trying to appear superior and innocent by making their partner look guilty.

Earlier in this part of the book, I said that many conversations and arguments turn into a sort of rivalry where two people are competing to be heard and understood. I said that had to change, and I suggested that you be the one to sheathe your metaphorical sword first. I suggested that instead of devoting your time, emotion and energy to clashing swords, you devote your time, emotion and energy to understanding and validating your partner's side of things.

If you're trying to cope with a spouse who tends to blame you for everything, that's the first approach I want you to take. Why? Because it's the least confrontational and also the lowest-conflict one. Plus, your partner won't be expecting this from you. When we've established an unpleasant dynamic or habit in our marriage, such as finger-pointing, it takes on a predictable nature. Spouses are always ready for a fight. Their hand is always on the hilt of their sword, so to speak. Your spouse will expect that once they blame you, you'll counter by blaming them. They expect that the harder they wield their sword, the harder you'll wield yours. What they are not expecting is that you'll step back, bow in good sportsmanship, and let them win the day. They're not ready for you to concede or, frankly, to care! So try that. Stop meeting your partner's resistant ways of communicating or interacting with your own resistant ways of communicating or interacting.

Break the habit of thinking, feeling, speaking and behaving in that "en garde" way. Instead, inject a peaceful gesture and spirit into those battle-ready dynamics and see if the outcome—that is, your spouse's reaction—is more peaceful. Put out a positive and peaceful (or at least not negative and warlike!) vibe on a personal level, and the overall vibe in your marriage will change.

Accept blame for what has happened (yes, even if you don't think it was your fault—what we're doing here is bigger than this one incident!) But don't stop at just accepting blame. Go a step further by acknowledging your partner's feelings and what they're going through. Acknowledge how your mistake has impacted them.

And then see what happens.

Let's re-visit our bickering couple on the way to the symphony. As they pull into the car park, the husband says, "Oh no, please tell me you remembered the tickets."

The wife throws up her hands. "No, I asked you to grab them."

"Did you?" says the husband. "Oh no, I must've been zoned out. I'm so sorry! I can't believe it. I know how much you were looking forward to tonight. And so was I. I'm really sorry. I've been really forgetful lately and now I've disappointed you. I feel awful, honestly."

Now, at this point, it's likely that the wife is going to be surprised—she wasn't expecting this from her husband. If the two of them are in the habit of blaming each other, she may be taken off guard when he lowers his guard! She might even stumble for words or with how to respond to him. It's like if you're madly clashing swords with someone and they suddenly step back and withdraw from the fight. That resistance isn't there anymore and it causes you to stumble to find your footing.

Yet this wife can only react in one of two ways, really. With any luck, she'll soften and say, "That's okay, these shoes are killing me anyway."

She might clue in to what her husband is doing, and if she's motivated to improve her marriage, she might recognize it as an opportunity to break their habit of pointing fingers. That might happen and that does happen quite often. It really is remarkable how little it sometimes takes to change those dynamics. When people love each other, they're often very receptive to any kind of olive branch.

Yet it's also possible that this wife will react in a less favorable way. If there's a lot of resentment, or if she's just really entrenched in her behavior, then she might use this as an opportunity to kick him while he's down. She might say, "Oh, I can't believe it! You're finally admitting that you're wrong about something. Amazing. I thought for sure you'd blame it on me, like you always do."

Yet here's the thing—and this is very, very important to know. Even if she does react negatively, selfishly, it's likely that at some point she is going to think back on this whole ordeal. She's going to remember that her husband accepted blame, and she's going to remember that she reacted in a really immature and destructive way.

In fact, it's in that post-conflict period that the real work is done. For many people who communicate in destructive ways, that is only time they are calm and humble enough to look at their own behavior.

A person who communicates in these unpleasant ways—with defensiveness or blaming—that person needs to get to the point that they're willing to look at their own behavior. And sometimes the best way to get them to that point is to remove ourselves from the equation.

When the husband blamed himself, he removed himself from the conflict. Now, the wife finds herself faced with having to respond to that. Typically, she'd react negatively by blaming him back, and that whole back and forth blame battle would go on for a while. Now she can't do that. So what will she do instead?

Like I said, maybe she won't do anything. Maybe she won't change—she'll just sit there, feeling satisfied with herself, and they'll go home. Or maybe, just maybe, she'll start to look at her own behavior.

Either way, the post-conflict period is, as far as her husband is concerned, a better place to be. At least there is the potential there that she will reflect upon her own behavior.

Just remember not to expect an instant change or positive response. It might take a few hours, it might take a few days, it might take a few weeks. But with any luck, your spouse will at some point sit back and think, "You know, maybe it was me who forgot the tickets. Maybe I shouldn't be so quick to blame him."

And that little spark of self-reflection can ignite some big changes in the way a couple communicates.

Couples who tend to blame each other for their problems also tend to communicate in some other fairly unhelpful ways. One of these is engaging in fact-based arguments.

"The tickets were on your desk!"

"No they weren't, they were on the kitchen counter."

That kind of thing. Except that it goes on and on and on. And even if you manage to win the argument by getting home and seeing the tickets were in fact on the desk, it won't make you feel any better, and it certainly won't make your spouse feel more love for you. It's a classic example of winning the battle but losing the war.

A couple like this may also be the kind who tends to moralize.

"You watch too much television. Don't you want to look at the real world instead of that stupid TV screen?"

"Oh yeah? Well, I might watch too much TV, but at least I don't smoke. Don't you want to be able to see the world without coughing up a lung?"

These communication habits are all interrelated. They tend to happen when one or both spouses feel the need to gain a foothold over the other. They want to be right and they want their partner to be wrong. They're nasty communication habits, but quite often they have more to do with the interactions and history of the marriage than poor communication skills per se.

They have more to do with the way spouses feel about each other. Do they feel heard, understood, loved and appreciated? Do they feel they can admit to a fault or shortcoming and their partner will receive that with humility and forgiveness?

There may be a lot going on under the surface with a person's who communicates in these ways. If you're struggling with these things, I recommend you revisit the section on decoding and understanding your spouse. Use that insight, combined with the communication strategies you've learned here, to see if you can break the cycle and get your partner to look at their own behavior.

And as with defensiveness, if you see any change whatsoever in your spouse's communication habits, if they accept blame for something or if they don't point fingers, make sure you let them know that you love them for that. Look for those opportunities, however small, and use them to your advantage.

Shine the spotlight on them: "I noticed that when we forgot the tickets, you took the fall for it. Thank you for that. It could've been either one of us that forgot, but it doesn't matter. I love you and I think you're amazing." In this way, your partner might just realize that winning your heart feels a lot better than winning an argument.

How to End the Silent Treatment

As if defensiveness and finger-pointing aren't enough to deal with, the silent treatment or the cold shoulder (essentially stonewalling), is a common tactic that's sometimes used during communication, or at least during poor communication.

It can be used by someone who just needs to cool off, which might be fair enough. It can be used when someone just doesn't know how else to communicate or handle conflict. But unfortunately, it can also be used as a deliberate way to hurt a spouse while simultaneously maintaining control over a situation.

When we talk about people who have short fuses, we often say that they throw an "adult temper tantrum" or an "adult fit." The phrase alludes to how childish the behavior appears. Well, the silent treatment is no better.

The thing is, when you behave in childish ways in your marriage, you create a childish marriage vibe. That's why the best way to deal with a spouse who uses the silent treatment, or any extreme behavior like this, is to always act like an adult regardless of whether they're choosing to do so or not.

If your partner uses the silent treatment, resist the urge to one-up them and think, *"Oh, you don't want to talk? Fine. I'll show you just how long I can go without saying a word!"* If you do that, the whole thing becomes a ridiculous competition. Never escalate your spouse's destructive communication habits with your own!

Instead, start by getting curious. Is there something you're doing that is causing your partner to shut down? Some spouses retreat into silence out of sheer frustration when they don't feel heard. If your partner tries to express a complaint or concern and they're met with anger, defensiveness or finger-pointing on your part, they may think, "What's the point of talking? They're not listening anyway." They may then use the cold shoulder as a way to hurt and ignore you, because they feel hurt and ignored by you.

Your partner may also shut down if you're bombarding them with questions, if you're talking too much or if you're pursuing them and aggressively or emotionally trying to get them to engage in conversation. Some people just don't know when to let it go—they'll just keep going at it, even if it's just descended into a pointless and heated argument that's been going on for way too long. Don't let that person be you.

So self-check. Is it possible that something you're doing is prompting your spouse to give you the silent treatment?

Let's say you've self-checked and think, "Nope, I'm good. It's them." Then what? How do you handle a spouse who gives you the silent treatment?

First, you have to understand why they do it. I've already given you some ways to try and figure that out (think decoding your spouse) and I've already run through some common reasons. Sometimes, people use the silent treatment or stonewall for the same reason they use short-fuse behavior or defensiveness: it can be a way to maintain control over a situation. Therefore, like those behaviors, it must be managed lest it undermine the healthy balance of power between spouses. Yet while it is manipulative behavior, it's important to know that not everyone who does this has chosen this path of communication in a conscious way—it might just be how they were taught, or how they learned, to get their needs met.

Regardless, they can be quite self-focused in the here and now, and that can create problems as they prioritize themselves, not their spouse. They can be preoccupied with what they are feeling or want to happen. Such spouses need to know that it isn't all about them, and that their behavior is taking a heavy toll on the way you feel about them.

After you've self-checked and tried to gain some insight into your spouse's behavior, you can begin by initiating a conversation about this issue with your partner. Make sure the timing, circumstances, and so on are as good as possible.

You can start with a fairly soft message by saying something like, "I know things are rough right now and we're both frustrated, but we need to keep some warmth between us. If you're angry with me, that's okay. We can work through it, but we have to work through it together. When you don't speak to me, it makes me feel unloved and afraid that we're drifting apart. What can I do to make it easier for you to talk to me?"

If your spouse responds in positive way, great. If after a reasonable time they haven't responded and the silence or stonewalling continues, you may have to increase the strength of your message by saying something along the lines of, "I'm not going to keep asking you what's wrong or coaxing you to talk. I'm doing my best, but I can't do this alone."

And then make sure you follow through with your words. Do *not* chase your partner around the house asking them to talk. Do not bend over backwards trying to be extra nice or comforting, hoping they'll crack.

I know that some people and practitioners may tell you to keep repeating that kind of question—What can I do to make it easier for you to talk?—but you must also avoid creating a habit where you're the one doing all the work, or where you're always prompting your partner to participate in their own relationship. Because unfortunately, that habit can and does develop.

By all means, do your best to make your spouse feel heard, try to understand them, tell them how you feel, be collaborative and ask what you can do to make things easier for them—but don't create a pattern where you do everything all the time. You don't want this behavior to pay off for them.

If your spouse doesn't respond to this or if they continue to use silence or stonewalling during other conversations or situations, then your message may need to get a little harder, and you may have to start putting some consequences in place.

You might want to say something like, "I love you, but it's too stressful to be near you when you refuse to talk to me. If we can't connect, then I think I'm going to move into the guest room for a while. I love you, and I know we can tackle any problem together, but we can't keep doing this. It's within our power to change, and we need to do that."

Does this sound dramatic to you? Maybe. But it's no more dramatic than weeks of silent tension.

And to be honest, this kind of behavior—as well as others, whether it's a short fuse or extreme defensiveness—is sometimes so habitual and entrenched that a person needs to see those real-world consequences before they feel motivated enough to make a change. Some people need to know that if they don't make a change, their spouse will make it for them. No, it's never ideal to get to this point. But that doesn't mean it never does.

Two things to mention here, though. The first is that you must remain in emotional control while doing this. If you're yelling or screaming or crying or generally behaving as badly as they are, they aren't going to take you seriously. We're talking about destructive communication habits and behaviors here—these are the kinds of things that can end a marriage if they go unchecked. That's why you need to approach this conversation with your spouse with gravity and sincerity. You shouldn't be rude, you should be resigned and respectful. Your spouse should be able to see the resignation and respect on your face and hear it in your voice.

And yet through it all, they should also be able to see and hear your willingness to collaborate and work with them to improve the communication and interactions in the marriage for both of you.

The second thing to remember is that whenever you issue a real-life consequence, such as saying you're going to sleep in the guest room, it can't be an empty threat. It has to be an intelligent and well-considered move, one that's basically a last resort, and it has to be one that you're ready, willing and able to follow through with, and that is appropriate in your circumstances.

So before you decide to implement this or any kind of real-world consequence, you must think about it long and hard. It can work, but it must be done at the right time, in the right way, and for the right reasons. It should also be a final recourse, after you've tried everything else and given it all time to work.

What to Do When Your Spouse Always Threatens Divorce

Another destructive communication habit is when a spouse threatens divorce during an argument. Sometimes, a spouse will do this when they don't feel that their partner is listening to them or taking them seriously. They might think, "I have to make a big noise here before they'll listen to me, so I'll threaten divorce, then they'll know I'm serious."

If your spouse does this, as always—and by now you should know what I'm going to say here—I want you to start by looking at your own behavior and communication habits. Do you ignore or dismiss your partner? If so, this could be their way of making that big noise and getting you to listen. So listen.

Yes, the behavior can come across as obnoxious, but sometimes it isn't. Sometimes it's cry for help. It's someone saying, "I love you, but I'm so hurt and fed up that you don't listen to me, that I'm pulling out all the stops." And when you look at it like that, you can see the stress and sadness under the words.

Yet a spouse who repeatedly threatens divorce may be doing this for the "shut up" factor. They're trying to get their partner to back down so that they can maintain control of the situation, by ending the conversation or avoiding a particular issue. In fact, you're likely beginning to see that, although destructive communication habits can look different, they're often caused by similar reasons and serve a similar purpose.

I suggest you handle this situation similar to the ways I outlined you handle the silent treatment. When the timing is right and you're both in a good, even happy place, talk to your spouse about this. Let them know the impact their behavior has on you and on the overall marriage. Threatening divorce when things get rough is the exact antithesis of everything marriage should be.

You can say something along the lines of, "When you threaten divorce, I feel like our marriage is unstable and built on weak ground. I feel like it isn't strong enough to withstand any problems. I hope that's not how you feel about us. If I'm doing something that's making you feel you have no other choice than to threaten divorce, let me know. I'll work on it. But please, don't disrespect our marriage by threatening to end it when we argue. "

If your spouse doesn't respond to this or continues to play the divorce card, do not respond. That is, don't allow them to think that their behavior is working. Avoid the pay off.

Don't beg them to stay, don't act afraid that they're going to leave, don't take back what you said or start apologizing for it. As long as you're confident that you're conducting yourself with humility and respect, then you're good.

Remember that people who communicate in belligerent or challenging ways usually have an end game—so don't play along. If your spouse realizes that their behavior isn't getting them anywhere and that you're not falling into line, they might drop it. If they see that you've become detached from their threats and they're just falling on deaf ears, they might stop issuing those threats.

Or they might not. And if they don't, then realistically, you have two choices. The first is to simply ignore it. Just let it slide off you, like water off a duck's back, as they say.

If they threaten divorce, simply interpret it as an empty threat and disregard it. But if that's your choice, there's no point asking them to stop doing it anymore. You'll only lose credibility and power as your partner realizes you aren't actually going to do anything about it. This isn't the choice I'd make, but it's your marriage and your choice. You need to do what's best for you.

Your second choice is to deliver that harder, last-resort message. The one that says I love, but there will be consequences if this continues (such as one spouse moving into the guest room).

If it comes to this, make sure that you remain in control of your emotions and that you deliver the message with confidence, but also with respect and a hope that things will change for the better.

And one more thing—a reminder, really. If you and your spouse have a conversation or an argument and they don't play the divorce card when they normally would, make sure you let them know that you noticed the change.

Shower them with praise, admiration and affection. Make them realize that biting their tongue can actually feel really good.

How To Handle an Emotional Onslaught
During Conversation

When most people think "emotional onslaught," they think of one of two things—anger or tears. That's definitely true. But it's also true that all of the destructive and challenging communication behaviors you've read so far—defensiveness, blaming, stonewalling, threatening divorce—can all be thought of as emotional onslaughts of one sort or another. They are all habits born of emotion that disrupt the healthy flow of conversation.

If you're the one who tends to emotionally overreact in one way or another during conversation, I suggest that you do four things.

First, revisit the section in part one of this book called What You Should STOP Doing Immediately, particularly the bits on short-fuse behavior and super-sensitivity. You need to know what's triggering you to do this.

Second, revisit the section here in part two called Peace Talks: How to Decode & Understand Your Spouse, and apply that exercise to yourself so that you can gain some insight into what's driving this behavior. Using the content in these two sections may help you get better self-control.

Third, talk to your spouse about it. As always, be sure to use the tips you learned in the Peace Talks sections so that you're choosing a good time to talk, and so on. Ask your spouse how the behavior makes them feel and react—once you hear from the horse's mouth (so to speak) how your behavior is affecting your spouse, you may find the motivation and strength to start getting it under control.

Finally, agree with your spouse that, if you start to escalate like this during conversation, you will disengage from the conversation as a couple. Give your spouse permission to end that conversation, albeit in a reassuring and respectful way. They might say something like, "Things are starting to get carried away. I love you, so let's do something else for a while and come back to this."

If it's your spouse who is displaying emotional onslaughts—whether anger, tears, or anything else—during conversation, you can employ a somewhat similar approach. I'll outline several steps here, although in the real world you may have to adapt these to suit your particular personalities and circumstances.

First, you're going to—as difficult as it might be to do this—try to emotionally disconnect and get curious for a moment. Try to understand / decode why they're behaving the way they are. What has triggered them? What is going on under the surface? Again, those sections I just mentioned will be helpful here.

Second, self-check. Is there anything you may be doing, even inadvertently, that is prompting them to react like this? Remember, this isn't blaming you for their behavior—they are completely responsible for their own behavior. Rather, this is just trying to understand and recognize how your respective conversational habits or other behaviors bounce off each other.

Third, talk to them. Acknowledge what they are feeling, and express your sincere desire to make the conversation more useful for them. They may simply need to feel heard.

Fourth, ask for their input. As you maintain your own emotional composure, ask your spouse what is going on with them, and/or what would make it easier for them to continue on with the conversation.

If you receive no useful feedback, you can express to your spouse how difficult it is for you to speak to them when they react in this way. If they are emotional, I advise against talking about this for too long. It's pointless and counterproductive to keep talking when someone is in this state. If you do, you'll likely end up as emotional as they are.

Instead, reassure your spouse that you love them. You can express your own feelings of sadness, or worry, or fear that the current conversation is harming the relationship more than helping it, and as a result, you wish to end the conversation. Then do it.

Reassure your spouse that you will continue the conversation at a later time (you can even pick a time if they require that kind of certainty). "Let's cool down for a half hour and then meet on the deck with a cup of tea to keep talking." That kind of thing.

Fifth, when the time, mood, environment and so on are suitable for a purposeful conversation, reconnect with your spouse to talk about the emotional onslaught behavior.

Be sure to employ everything you've learned so far in this book, both from part one and this part. Be sure to pick and choose those strategies, including those from the Peace Talks sections, that you think can help you move the conversation along in a positive way. Yes, there will be some trial and error involved. These insights and strategies are solid, but you and your spouse are unique people, with a unique relationship and habits, and you'll have to see what works best, adapting as you go.

Sixth, when the conversation is over, be sure to show your spouse appreciation and gratitude for their willingness to talk about this, and to work on this behavior. If they are open to it, show them the content in this book or ask them to find their own or a different resource if that works better for them.

Do something enjoyable together at the end of this kind of conversation, whether it's going out for supper or making a tray of cheesy nachos and watching a funny movie at home. Always balance the heavy with the light.

Now, let's say you try to do all of this, but your spouse just isn't open to it. Despite your best efforts and self-checking, they just won't budge in terms of their behavior, and you suspect they are behaving in this way to maintain control over the conversation or the situation (whether consciously or not). Then what?

Then you're back to those two choices I mentioned in the previous section. You can either choose to live with the behavior (perhaps it's rare, fleeting and not severe, and you feel your spouse's good qualities outweigh it) or you can institute some kind of consequence.

The example I gave is having one of you move into the guest room. After all, if you can't communicate, then you can't connect, and you can't really be intimate anyway. Another consequence might be insisting that you receive professional help as a couple from whatever resource you feel is right for you.

If you choose to institute some kind of consequence, be sure that you're actually ready to take that step, and that you can do so in a way that is respectful, realistic and safe. As always, you must use your own judgment, as well as your knowledge of your spouse and circumstances, when deciding how to proceed.

Communication Landmines & How to Sidestep Them

Many of the destructive communication habits I've covered in this part of the book are tough behaviors to deal with. They're confusing, too. I've presented a number of insights and strategies, and I'm confident they'll help you approach your communication struggles from some new angles, whether you're behaving in these ways or whether your spouse is doing it (or whether it's a bit of both depending on the issue and the day!).

Yet before we leave part two, there are three additional and very common communication mistakes that I want to cover. These are some of the worst communication landmines out there. Why do I call them landmines? Because you don't typically know that they're there! You might be stepping on these landmines every single day without evening knowing it. And believe me, they can cause a lot of damage.

This first communication landmine is **repetition**. Stop repeating yourself! A spouse who feels unheard will often express the same concerns or feelings over and over again, hoping that at some point their partner will acknowledge what they're saying and show insight or reassure them.

They may repeatedly remind their partner of something—remember it's your turn to cook dinner...remember to pick up the kids...remember to pay the bills... But no matter how many times they repeat the reminder, their partner forgets every time. So they remind them again, hoping that at some point their partner will remember.

That's unlikely. What's more likely is that your partner will begin to tune you out. They'll also start to see you as a nag. Even worse, you may start to feel like a nag. And nobody wants to feel that way. It feels powerless and degrading, and it can lead to a lot of resentment on the part of both spouses.

If this resonates with you, I urge you to adopt a "no-repeat policy" in your own mind. Say what you need to say once or twice, then no more. Ask for what you want once or twice, then no more. Trust me, this is far more likely to motivate your partner to listen. I know it seems counterintuitive, but the moment you stop repeating yourself is often the same moment that your spouse will open their ears.

Why? Because when you stop repeating yourself, you're doing something unexpected. Your partner is fully expecting you to keep saying the same things, to keep reminding them of the same things, and to keep asking them the same things, probably even using the same words and tone of voice.

When you stop repeating yourself, they notice, since you are creating a void that your repetition would normally fill. That's going to catch their attention faster than yet another repeated reminder, complaint or request.

The second communication landmine is **excessive explanation**. Of course, we all need to explain ourselves from time to time. But we don't need to explain ourselves excessively. Yet spouses who are frustrated, or who feel unheard, often do verbal gymnastics trying to find yet another way to explain to their spouse why they're unhappy or why they see a certain situation the way they do.

You might think, "How can my partner not understand this?" So you keep trying to explain it to them. You think, "If I just choose the right words, if I just show the right emotion, if I can just catch them in the right mood, they'll understand! The light will go on and they'll get it! They'll understand why I feel the way I do and they'll agree with me."

Know this: If you've already explained yourself, it is very likely that your partner completely understands how you feel or why you're hurt or angry. It's very likely they already understand your complaints and what you want from them.

So stop explaining yourself. If you feel in your heart that you've already explained yourself very well in terms of your feelings, opinions or requests, then don't do it again. Doing so only drains you of power and energy, and fills you with frustration and heartache.

There is an arsenal of other strategies in this book that can help you connect with your spouse. So instead of continuing to do what isn't working, such as repeating yourself or excessively explaining yourself, try something new.

The third and final communication landmine I want to touch on is **talking about your problems—and nothing else.** Many couples who are fighting to get along fall into an unhappy habit of only talking about their problems.

Every time one spouse opens their mouth the other spouse knows what's going to come out—something to do with the marriage and what's wrong with it.

Please, don't let every word you utter be about your marriage problems! Find something else to talk about. Rediscover the lost art of conversation. Sit in a café and talk about a good book over a great cup of coffee. Don't just talk at each other—talk *with* each other.

Sit in a shopping mall or on a bench downtown and do some people watching. Challenge each other to analyze the couples you see. That couple picking out the latest phone: are they married or dating? That couple standing in line to enter the new five-star restaurant: what's their story?

Take an evening stroll and look up at the stars. Is there life on other planets? Would you be among the first to colonize Mars if you could? Talk about it. Watch a controversial film—do you like it or hate it? Go to an art museum—what would you hang over the fireplace, and what would you burn in it?

Engage each other in true conversation—conversation that has nothing to do with work, or your bills, or the kids, or chores, or your marriage problems. Have the kind of conversation that two friends who are interested in each other and who have interesting things to talk about would have.

Remember that the purpose of communication isn't just to help you talk through your problems. The purpose is to connect and stay connected. So do your part to revive the lost art of conversation. It'll bring some much-needed civility to your discourse and to your marriage.

WORKING THROUGH IT, PART TWO

Peace Talks: Diplomatic Discussions

Think about how you and your spouse communicate: do you compete to be heard, or do you compete to hear the other person? Does that "let me go first" setting factor into conversation? Think of an example.

How might shifting this habit or dynamic to a "you go first" setting change things? Imagine a scenario where you do that: what might happen?

If you are hesitant to make this shift, why? (e.g. you feel too much resentment, you feel your spouse won't give you the same priority treatment, etc.)

If you were to make this shift, even on your own, how might it change the way you talk?

If you were to make this shift, how might your spouse respond?

Peace Talks: Gathering Intelligence

If you and your spouse are fighting to get along, go through the ten questions in this section and answer them to the best of your ability. After you have answered those questions, summarize what you learned.

Do you feel this has helped you understand your spouse better? How so?

How will you use what you learned in a practical way? That is, how can you use this information to improve the way you interact and communicate?

How might this kind of intelligence gathering affect the way you communicate with your spouse?

How might your spouse respond if you were to begin doing this?

Using what you learned in this section, are there areas of your marriage you think you can improve without having another conversation about it?

Peace Talks: How to Decode & Understand Your Spouse

Does your spouse ever say things or behave in ways you don't understand? Be specific.

Using the cross-section approach in this section, can you decode your spouse to see what might be going on under the surface of their words, statements, or behavior?

Think of a common or recurrent conflict or argument between you and your spouse. Without asking your spouse to explain themselves, use the cross-section approach in this section to see whether you can better understand their side of things.

Peace Talks: How to Express Yourself Without Starting a War

Do you ever say, "I don't know" when your spouse is trying to get information from you? If so, why?

If you truly don't know why you are reacting in certain ways or feel a certain way about something, revisit the cross-section exercise in the previous section to "decode" yourself.

How might knowing yourself better (and thus avoiding saying "I don't know") improve communication between you and your spouse?

Peace Talks: How to Have a Fabulous Conversation About Anything

What topic or issue do you wish to discuss with your spouse?

What steps can you take, before that happens, to ensure the conversation is as successful as possible?

Peace Talks: The Secret Weapons of Fabulous Communication

Which of the strategies in this section seem like they would be the most useful to you?

Think of an issue you and your spouse typically argue about. How might employing these strategies help you discuss it more pleasantly?

Keeping the Peace: The Power of Micro Talks

Think of an issue you and your spouse have recently discussed. Is there a way you can use micro talks to keep you on track in terms of addressing that issue? Be specific.

How to Break Through Defensiveness

Recall a time when your spouse became defensive during conversation. Replay the scenario in your mind. Now, brainstorm how you might have:

• Addressed the issue indirectly to avoid triggering your spouse's defensive reaction

• Addressed the issue directly through conversation (write down the steps you would have taken to do this in a positive, fair, low-conflict way)

If your spouse tends to be defensive, why do you think they typically react in that way? You may wish to return to the decoding exercise.

Does your spouse receive any kind of "payoff" for reacting defensively? How can you avoid that?

How to Stop Pointing Fingers

If your spouse tends to play the blame game during conversation or conflict, how might you inject a peaceful gesture into those battle-ready dynamics?

How might your spouse respond to that?

How to End the Silent Treatment

If your spouse tends to stonewall during conversation, why do you think they do so?

After reading this section, how might you approach this situation differently?

How to Handle an Emotional Onslaught During Conversation

Do you tend to react emotionally—that is, emotionally enough to disrupt the normal flow of conversation—when communicating with your spouse? If so, why?

If you're the one who tends to display these kinds of behaviors, how can you work with your spouse to reduce the behavior?

If it is your spouse who tends to display these kinds of behaviors, what do you think is behind the behavior (you may wish to get curious about their triggers or to decode them)?

Might you be inadvertently contributing to this behavior? How so?

What can you do to help your spouse reduce these behaviors?

If your spouse refuses to change these behaviors, what will you do?

Communication Landmines & How to Sidestep Them

Are you inadvertently stepping on any of the communication landmines in this section? Which ones, specifically?

Do a little self-reflection. Why are you behaving like this?

Looking at each communication landmine in turn, how might sidestepping it change the way you communicate? How might your spouse respond when you sidestep these things?

PART THREE:

How to "Fight Nice": Resolve Conflict and Get On With Life

Fight Nice, You Two!

When my sister and I were kids and would start arguing about something, our mom would stick her head in the room and always say the same thing—"Fight nice, you two."

It was one of those mom-isms that always irked me. And yet now, if I hear my husband and son arguing about something, I'll say the same thing—"Fight nice, you guys."

It's a handy little saying, because it says a lot in just two words—*fight nice*. It releases the pressure of an escalating argument and reminds people to keep their perspective. It reminds them that their relationship is more important than whatever passing triviality they're arguing about. It places value on the integrity of the relationship and prioritizes it.

The truth is, couples will always argue. They'll always fight. But if they can learn to "fight nice," then conflict will always remain at a manageable, respectful, even purposeful level. There is absolutely no reason why a couple cannot learn to use conflict to their advantage—as a way to learn more about each and their relationship, and to make their marriage stronger instead of weaker. Every conflict that a couple successfully navigates, whether it's a snide remark in the kitchen or a heated argument behind closed bedroom doors, can actually ensure that their marriage remains a happy one in the long-term.

As we move now into part three of this book, I will remind you again to regularly review what you learned in parts one and two, especially those sections that you found particularly relevant and useful. If you've made notes, perhaps adapting these insights or strategies to your unique situation, be sure to review those, too.

In fact, if you've made good use of parts one and two, it's very likely that this part of the book won't be quite as critical as you think. You'll recall that this book's three-part structure is designed to have a cumulative effect.

Once you improve the interactions in your relationship (the way you treat each other), much of your verbal communication (the way you talk to each other) naturally improves.

And once you improve both your interactions and your communication, you'll find that a lot of the underlying conflicts in your relationship—all that stuff you argue about—just kind of fades away. Not all of it, but a lot of it. Parts one and two can be quite transformative and can equip spouses to interact and communicate in far more sophisticated and successful ways. When problems arise— as they always will—these spouses are far better able to manage them quickly and effectively.

Yet even successful couples can still find themselves faced with serious conflict now and then. Sometimes, they can even fall into a pattern of pointless arguing or fighting to get along. If that's you, you'll find this part of the book very helpful.

Plus, there will always be problems that will require targeted management. Money is one. Yes, it's great to talk about your spending habits, but you still need to put your heads together and create an actual budget that works for both of you.

Housework is another issue. Yes, it's great to want to work together in terms of household chores, but life is messy and busy and you may need to do some practical designating.

Yet another area is socializing and lifestyle. Yes, it's fantastic if you and your spouse can get on the same page here, but what exactly does that mean in terms of socializing with opposite-sex friends, or using technology in the home or arranging your schedules so you both have time to engage in outside interests or go out with friends?

It's in this part that you'll learn how to negotiate and agree on what to do, especially if you still have different opinions or preferences, even after you've talked it through. Every successful couple must be able to resolve conflict.

This part of the book also revisits some challenging behavior that I touched on previously: that is, how to manage particularly uncooperative spouses (e.g. defensive, blaming, indifferent or immature, self-centered). In parts one and two, I encouraged you to look at your own behavior to make sure you're not doing these things or contributing to these behaviors on the part of your spouse. I gave you some practical strategies to help you manage these uncooperative behaviors and communication habits on the part of your spouse so that both of you could have better conversation.

Yet some spouses are very entrenched in these behaviors and it seems like no matter what you say or do, or how you say or do it, you just can't seem to reach them or prompt them to change. That can make it really hard to get to the point where you can actually resolve an issue or conflict with them. These kinds of partners may not respond to the techniques I've presented earlier, so I'll give you additional tools to try here.

Finding Common Ground

It was in the years before I founded Marriage SOS, when I still worked as a divorce mediator, that I received a lot of my early experience with higher-conflict situations and people. Many times, I would find myself in a room with two people who were at each other's throats. You could physically feel the anger and animosity between them. Emotions were high and volatile. To put it bluntly, these people couldn't stand each other, and that was simmering just under the surface. Yet my job was to get them to a point where they could have a civil conversation and at least sit in the same room without shooting lasers out of their eyes at each other.

But how to do that? Well, it largely depended on the couple and what vibe I got from them. Sometimes, I just trudged through relying solely on my training and playing it by the book.

Other times, I'd get a different sense from the couple...like they were willing and open, even eager, to have some kind of meaningful connection despite the divorce. These couples often had children together, so that's where I'd typically start. I'd ask them their kids' names, how old they were, whether they liked superheroes, that kind of thing. Small talk. I'd steer clear of the big issues like living arrangements or child-support payments, and instead I'd try to get them to experience a shared memory or emotion about their kids. I'd try to lead them to some kind of common ground.

And then I'd use that. If the circumstances and the personalities of the people I was dealing with permitted it, I'd use that common ground to bring them just a few steps closer together.

I might gently remind them that everything they were doing right now, in that room, they were doing for their kids. They were ending their relationship as husband and wife, but they were still honoring the obligation they had to the children as co-parents. In many situations, this was the one glimmer of light in a very dark place. It was the one patch of common ground, the one shared interest, between two people who otherwise thought of each other as the enemy.

I want you to think about that. Finding some kind of common ground is one of the first and one of the best ways to manage a conflict situation. So that's what I want you to do.

This requires a shift in thinking. Let me explain: When most of us approach conflict, we do so in a positional way. We have our position, which might be the way we think or feel about something, the opinion we have about something, or the outcome we're looking for. That's our position.

Conflict happens because our spouse is doing the same thing—although they're typically taking a different position! They have a different thought or feeling or opinion, and they might be looking for a different outcome.

When these two positions clash—that is, when we argue or fight—we're basically digging our heels deeper into our own respective positions.

And then what happens? Well, the same thing that probably happens in your kitchen or living room or bedroom. You become entrenched in your position and you fight harder for it. Defensiveness, blow-ups, cold shoulders, blaming, fact-based arguments, criticism and assumptions—all these weapons of marriage destruction start destroying the love between you.

To prevent that from happening, you need to make a mental shift from defending your position to finding common ground.

Step back from your position and think, "Okay, I'm pretty clear here about our differences—our different feelings or opinions—but what about our similarities? Is there any common ground between us? Do we have any shared interests?"

By shared interests, I don't just mean the things that both of you like, like disco music or zombie movies or guacamole. It's a little deeper than that. I mean, what values, needs, fears or other factors do you both deeply, deeply care about? Shared interests are those fundamental things that connect us, and that can motivate us to work through our problems in a collaborative and positive way. These are the ties that bind.

So ask yourself: What is the common ground between us? What are our shared interests?

Well, you're married and you love each other. That's a shared interest. That's common ground. And I absolutely 100% guarantee that you have other shared interests, too.

Do you argue about money? Even if you have different spending habits, you have a shared interest—to keep a roof over your head and a set of wheels in the driveway!

Do you argue about parenting or your kids? Even if you have different parenting styles, you have a shared interest—to raise independent, healthy and well-adjusted children who will be happy and successful in life.

Do you argue about anything and everything? You have a shared interest—to create a loving and low-conflict marriage that provides both of you with intimate companionship, security, joy and well-being in life. You have a shared interest to have a marriage that models for your kids what a happy, healthy, long-term relationship looks like, and which provides a low-stress home so they can truly enjoy those fleeting and carefree years of childhood.

When you look at it like that, your shared interests are far more important and powerful than your differences. So use that. Use that to bring a sense of solidarity to your marriage and to the way you approach conflict. Look for the values you share. Look for the needs or perhaps more specifically the unfulfilled needs that both you share. Look for the fears that both of you share.
Use those to bring you closer.

How do you do that, exactly? For starters, by identifying your shared interests and talking about them. By spending less time talking about your differences and hurt feelings and the things you're mad or disappointed about, and more time talking about the things you have in common—your values, your needs, your fears and your hopes.

Spouses who find themselves fighting to get along tend to go through their days and their marriage with a constant low-level of tension and antagonism. They're keenly aware of their enemy status, but by devoting more emotion and energy to focusing on what binds you, instead of what divides you, you'll find yourselves in a much better place to solve your problems. You'll find yourselves more motivated to solve your problems, and to do that in a collaborative instead of antagonistic way.

I remember working with a long-time married couple who were fighting about everything—lots of nasty interactions, always walking on eggshells around each other, that kind of thing. There wasn't one major area of conflict, just a thousand little things.

One of the thousand things they were fighting about was their very old cat I mean *very* old cat He was one of those immortal cats that you read about in Guinness World Records. I think it was pushing twenty-five years old or something like that. This cat's name was the King. Anyway, the King was starting to have a number of serious health issues, age-related issues obviously, and that was starting to impact his quality of life. So that big question was hanging over their heads—when is it the right time to have him put to sleep?

This couple had booked euthanasia appointments three or four times with the vet clinic, but each time one of them would call and cancel, saying they weren't ready. Now, this couple's shared interest is obvious—they both loved the King. They both wanted to do the right thing for him and they wanted to make sure the timing was right: *Are you sure there are no more good days left for him?* But it didn't take me long to find another shared interest, and this one was a little deeper under the surface.

As it turned out, they had adopted the King the day that they both moved into their first apartment together. They each told the story the same way. They had gone looking for a "baby" at the local animal shelter. It was a hard choice—if you've ever been to animal shelter you know that—but they turned a corner and saw the kitten King, and at the moment they met eyes, they heard Elvis Presley's song *Jailhouse Rock* over the shelter's speaker system and thought, "That's the one. It's a sign. Let's spring him."

The King wasn't just a cat to this couple. He was the tie that bound them and that wove throughout their lives. They had him when they moved into their first apartment, they had him when they bought their first house, and they had him when their children were born. He was there as their kids grew up, photobombing every family picture they took. He was there when their kids went off to college and once again it was just the two of them and their cat.

He was a symbol of their shared history, their very identity as a couple. He was that constant in their lives. They didn't call themselves his owners, they called themselves his subjects. And they both were afraid of the same thing. *When the King is gone, are we gone?* They had the same unspoken but shared fear—that losing their cat was like losing a little bit of their history and identity. And since things weren't great in the marriage anyway, that fear was really amplified.

Anyway, I really like cats and I really liked this couple, so I asked the wife to email me a photo of the King, just so I could see him. He was a bit of a legend, so I was curious. When she did, I did a little editing and sent the photo back with the words "The King commands his subjects to be loyal to each other" on it.

As it happened, the King did shuffle off his mortal coil a few days after that, and his departure did mark a turning point for this couple. As I spoke to them about it, they realized that they were both afraid of the same thing—of drifting apart, of losing their history and identity, of going through life separately instead of together.

And that realization turned the tide so that instead of constantly focusing on conflict, they started focusing more on connecting. Instead of locking horns and resisting each other, they began to work together to solve their problems.

That's that shift I was talking about earlier—the shift from simply defending your respective positions, to looking for common ground and shared interests. You have them. I guarantee you have them. So find them and let them be the ties that bind. Let them provide a lifeline that you can use to pull yourself out of conflict and into collaboration.

Every time you feel yourself being pulled into conflict, into some back and forth argument or tension, make that mental shift—focus less on your different positions and focus more on your shared interests.

Find that common ground and stand on it. Remain standing on it as you talk through your problems. This fundamental shift in the way you approach conflict can create a wonderfully collaborative spirit between spouses.

The Paths to Peace

Moving on, I want to spend a few minutes talking about your options when it comes to resolving conflict in marriage. You can think of these as general paths to peace. As we move forward in this part of the book, I'm going to get a lot more specific, but right now, let's just look at your four overarching options.

The first option to resolving conflict in a practical and real-world way is to simply **handle it by yourself**. This is when you, working alone, take steps to resolve the conflict on your own.

The best way to do this in a proactive and positive way is to think back to the section on gathering intelligence in part two, where I prompted you to ask yourself a series of questions about your partner. The goal was for you to figure out what is bothering your spouse on your own, without needing to have a big talk or conversation about it.

That's because much of time partners already know each other's complaints. Sometimes we've been listening to our spouse express them for weeks or months or even years. The case I mentioned in that section involved a wife who knew her husband was bothered by the kids leaving their tablet on the floor and not doing their chores...so instead of once again asking her husband why he was upset, she took it upon herself to make sure the kids did their chores and put the tablet away safely. Problem solved. That's handling it yourself, and it's as simple as it gets.

Sometimes, we can read our partner's mind. Sometimes it's more effective to simply address their recurring and reasonable complaints on our own, instead of talking about it again. So do that.

Best-guess your partner's complaints or concerns, and then take steps, on your own, to address those. Not only does this spare you yet another big talk about what's wrong with the marriage, but it shows your partner that you're willing to take the lead—and that can lead to some very good things.

The second general option to resolving conflict is to **take one for the team**. You know what this expression means: it means you will accept something, or make some kind of sacrifice, even if it's a little unpleasant, for the greater good. For example, you might prevent an argument from escalating by just letting your partner have their way or just doing what they want.

Now, this might not initially sound like a good idea, but it definitely has its place. When you look at the big picture of your marriage, it can spare you a lot of pointless arguing.

Let's say you're going out for supper. You want Italian, but your spouse feels like Greek. In some marriages, especially ones where spouses are fighting to get along, this nice evening is going to descend into an argument.

"We always do what you want to do!"

"No, we always do what you want to do!"

Maybe. Or maybe it's just supper.

Unless there's a real reason not to, why not just let your spouse have their way? Just say, "Sure, Greek sounds great. Some coffee and baklava? What could be better." If it isn't a big deal, don't make it a big deal.

Are you going to do this every time? Of course not. That's not what I'm saying. What I'm saying is that taking one for the team—that is, making some minor sacrifice in the course of your day to keep the peace—isn't always a bad thing. We all want to have our way at times and sometimes it just isn't worth an argument.

When faced with a situation where you want one thing and your partner wants another, just ask yourself: *Self, is this the hill I want to die on? Is this a big deal?*

Believe it or not, taking one for the team—you can think of it as concession, or giving in—can produce some very good vibes in a marriage. It shows your spouse that you care about their interests and preferences, and that you have a self-sacrificing spirit. And you'll remember that having a self-sacrificing spirit is one of those positive personality traits I talked about in part one.

Remember also that displaying positive personality traits and behaviors can prompt your spouse to display their own positive personality traits and behaviors. Your spouse sees what you're doing, and they like it. That can only lead to good things.

The third option is **compromise**. Simply understood, this is when spouses reach an agreement by each of them giving in or conceding to some extent. They meet in the middle, so to speak.

You've probably heard people talk about how important compromise is within marriage. That's true to some extent. Let's say a couple is house shopping. They both want a house that's in a certain neighborhood. In addition, the wife wants a house that has a big backyard, while the husband wants a two-car garage. However, it's a seller's market, and there isn't a lot of inventory to choose from. The houses that are for sale in their preferred neighborhood either have a big yard or a big garage, but not both.

So they compromise. They buy a house in their preferred neighborhood, but it has a pretty small yard and only a one-car garage. Despite the compromise, it's likely that every time the wife looks at the yard she'll think, "This is a small yard" and every time the husband pulls into the garage he'll think, "This is a small garage."

It may be that both of them can live with that. If the primary consideration for both partners was to buy a house in that specific neighborhood, then they'll probably be satisfied with their purchase and won't have any regrets under the circumstances. So compromise can be a really good option, and in some situations, it's the only option.

However, it might be that **collaboration**, which is the fourth option I want to mention, is a better approach here. With collaboration, both spouses keep working at it until both are completely satisfied with the outcome.

And that's different than compromise, where both spouses may sometimes be only *partly* satisfied with the outcome—that is, neither one is getting exactly what they want.

Collaboration requires a little more thought and investigation, a little more exploration of what each person wants and why they want it, and a little more brainstorming.

Let's return to our house-shopping couple. If this couple had a collaborative spirit, they would sit down and hammer it out. They would talk it through, and ask each other why they wanted a big yard or a big garage.

They may discover that the wife only wanted a big yard for two reasons: the first was to let their dog get more exercise. This couple has come from an apartment, and she wants her dog to have more room to move. Her second reason is that she wants to have a backyard garden. She has lived in apartments her entire life, and having a vegetable garden has always been a dream of hers.

The husband wants a big garage for fairly obvious reasons. They live in a northern climate, and he wants both of them to be able to park in the garage so they don't have to dig their cars out of the snow every winter morning.

Armed with this insight, this couple can now house-shop with their respective needs in mind. They're more flexible and open minded, and they are more likely to get creative in terms of resolving this issue.

As it turns out, they find a beautiful house in their preferred neighborhood. It has a big two-car garage, but it doesn't have a big yard; however, it is located beside a gorgeous walking trail that leads to a huge green space. It's only steps away from their back door— it's perfect! Not only can the wife run the dog every morning, but the location actually adds a lot of value to the home.

The house also has a very large wraparound deck that provides the ideal location for a raised vegetable garden. And the more the wife thinks about it, the more she loves that idea. It'll be easy to maintain and it'll look really stylish on the deck.

That's collaboration. Both spouses are completely happy with the outcome. There's no kind-of happy or half-happy, they're both 100% happy. Of course, collaboration isn't always possible. There will be situations and circumstances where the other options—handling it yourself, taking one for the team, and compromising—will have to work, and will work just fine.

That being said, whenever you can, I want you to approach conflict with a **collaborative spirit**. With an open mind.

When you find yourselves arguing about something or stuck in conflict, do what this house-shopping couple did—do some investigation and dig a little deeper so that you can understand the *reasons* underlying your respective positions.

Instead of digging your heels in and saying, "I want this" and "I want that," slow down and get curious about why each of you actually wants what you do. When you expand your thinking like this, you increase the chances that you'll both get exactly what you want, and then some.

Stop the Insanity: How to End 90% of Fights

I was once in a class where we had a guest speaker, a fairly eccentric chap, who was to speak to us about conflict resolution principles and various interpersonal dynamics. As the class was getting seated, he announced that he was just slipping out to grab a cup of coffee and he'd be right back when, instead of exiting through the door, he walked into the wall about a foot away from the door. He did this about five times…it took two or three times for the class to clue in to the fact that he was doing it on purpose, and not just stumbling en route to a cup of coffee to sober up.

"This is what people do," he said. "They keep hitting their head against the wall in the same spot. What should I do?" he asked, and someone shouted, "Move to the left, man!" and so he did, and slipped out the doorway to get his coffee.

Perhaps you've heard Einstein's definition of insanity: It's doing the same thing over and over again and expecting different results. We all do this, and we especially do it in our interpersonal relationships. Many couples who find themselves fighting to get along say that their days are filled with nasty, pointless little arguments that can become an all too familiar habit of behavior in the marriage. No matter how hard they try to avoid them, it seems like they always end up traveling down that same road that leads to some kind of bickering or fight.

Picture this. You're driving in your car when you realize you're lost; however, you do recognize the road you're on. You were just on it a few minutes ago, and it led to a dead end. So let me ask you: Do you keep driving forward?

That is, do you keep heading toward the dead end, perhaps hoping that, in the five minutes since you were last there, some magical construction crew descended from the clouds and built a highway that leads straight to your destination?

Of course not. That would be foolish. You know where the road leads—to a dead end. You know nothing has changed. So you change course. You start driving in a different direction.

In what direction and to where? I don't know. Maybe to the left. But maybe it doesn't matter. Maybe what matters is that you won't hit that same dead end. If you're lucky, maybe you'll stumble across a gas station or a nice restaurant or a great hotel on this new road. Regardless, anything and anywhere is better than the dead end. In fact, I'd be willing to bet you can remember a time when taking an unexplored road led you and your spouse to an amazing place.

I'm beating the metaphor to death, but you get where I'm going with this. If you fall into conflict with your spouse—whether it's a loud argument or silent fuming—and you recognize the familiar path you're on, then I want you to simply drive off the path. Stop hitting your head against the same spot on the wall and instead move to the left! Or the right. Whatever. The idea is to break the habit and take a different path. Any path, as long as it doesn't lead to the same dead end and the same pointless argument or conflict. Honestly, this is just common sense. You know this. You already do this in other areas of your life. so do it in your marriage, too.

When you do, you'll get a big payoff—a pleasant, affirming rush of hope! When you feel the joy of the open road instead of the letdown of the dead end, you feel good! And best of all, you'll want to keep going forward. There's no risk of someone saying, "Nothing will ever change!" and then bailing from the car to run off into the hills.

Let's look at this changing course strategy in action. Take the case of a couple who has the same fight every day after supper.

The moment they are finished eating, the wife stands up and says, "Let's clean off the table."

The husband rolls his eyes, rubs his stomach and says, "Oh come on, let's relax and watch a little television first. It'll wait."

The wife lets out an exasperated sigh. "You know I can't relax until the table is cleaned off!"

At that, the husband starts grabbing things off the table and, in an obviously irritated mood, shoves plates and glasses into the dishwasher. His wife, also now irritated, sighs again and reorganizes the dishwasher.

"The dishes won't come clean if you load them like that," she gripes. "How many times do I have to tell you the same thing?"

You can guess how the rest of this couple's evening is going to go.

Now, let's see how this couple might change course to avoid the same negative, nowhere dead end argument.

The moment they are finished eating, the wife stands up and says, "Let's clean off the table."

The husband rolls his eyes, rubs his stomach and says, "Oh come on, let's relax and watch a little television first. It'll wait."

The wife thinks "change course." Instead of falling into the habitual argument they always have, she recognizes the path ahead of her, and she veers off course before she hits the dead end.

By sheer force of will, she smiles and says, "You're right. Let's go snuggle on the couch for a while. I missed you today."

Not only has this detour steered them clear of their usual argument, but the wife's unexpected behavior has caught her husband's attention, and in a very good way. He knows that she likes to clean off the table before relaxing, so her agreement to watch some television first means a lot to him. He knows it isn't easy for her and that she is doing it to avoid the argument. As a result, the evening is far more likely to be an enjoyable one. The husband may change his mind and say, "That is very sweet of you, but let's clear the table now so you can relax." That is, he may try to return the favor. Or perhaps they will just snuggle on the couch and enjoy being close. Either way, the wife has cancelled their regularly scheduled 6:43 pm argument. That has already made a difference.

I want you to be on high alert for these predictable, well-worn, and familiar paths of conflict in your marriage. Watch out for those dead ends. When you know you're on the road to one, stop in your tracks and change course. Change direction. Prove to your spouse, and to yourself, that things can change for the better in your marriage. You're behind the wheel, so start acting like it.

You may be surprised by how many arguments and fights you can avoid by using this simple but Einstein-inspired strategy— stop the insanity of doing the same thing over and over again, and expecting a different result. Instead, crank that wheel in a different direction. A saner direction. Once you start doing this, you and your spouse may find yourselves in some amazing new places.

If you've read any of my other books, you may remember the term "defamiliarization." Simply put, this is the concept of presenting what is familiar in an unfamiliar way.

Defamiliarization is an idea I utilize a lot in my practice, and you can think of this strategy as a form of it, too. By taking an unfamiliar path or behaving in an unfamiliar way, you create a situation where you are compelled to see, feel, and experience things from a different perspective. That creates a kind of "shake up" within a marriage that can produce great results. So keep this concept in mind. Whenever you can detour away from a familiar path of conflict, make sure you do it. It's the sane thing to do!

Your Target: What You're REALLY Fighting About

Have you ever said the words, "I don't even know what we're fighting about" or "We fight about anything and everything"? Many couples say they're bombarded with constant mini fights—a squabble here, a squabble there, a squabble everywhere.

Others say they keep it all inside until it blows up. So there is a period of uneasy calm followed by an eruption, followed by another uneasy calm and another eruption, over and over again. It's the marital equivalent of living at the base of an active volcano.

Regardless of your specific conflict habits or dynamics, it's very likely that your arguments leave you feeling emotionally drained and a bit baffled. Why are we fighting all the time? The answer is this: you haven't gotten to the root of your arguments.

You've heard that expression: *Getting to the root of the problem.* To the root of the argument. It's true, and you need to do it. It's like this: Every now and then, I'll have a client who sits down in front of me and who and begins to list off all the complaints they have about their spouse, and all the fights they've had.

They'll talk about how their spouse doesn't respond to texts, how they walk across the floor with their muddy boots on, how they don't spend enough time with their kids, how they don't show as much interest in sex, how they're rude or thoughtless, how they don't help with housework, how they overspend, how they forget birthdays or anniversaries, or how they micromanage them....

It's like a grocery list of complaints, and they're walking down every aisle, throwing everything into the cart.

When I have a client like this, I'll usually stop them after a couple minutes. I'll get up, walk to the big whiteboard on my office wall, and I'll draw a big tree on it. This tree has a lot branches and a lot of leaves, but only a few really big roots.

Then, I'll hand the marker to my client—let's say it's a husband—and I'll say, "Okay, I want you to label each branch and each leaf. Each one is a complaint you have about your wife, or a fight or argument you've had. Go ahead, get it all out. Write down everything you can think of."

So this husband does just that. He starts labeling the branches with his complaints about his wife, as well as the things they've argued or fought about recently. He writes down things like: my wife never responds to my texts, she isn't interested in sex, she's spending a lot of money lately, she forgot about our anniversary...the list goes on.

After he's finished, I'll say, "Do you remember that grade school exercise where you had to group similar things together? Like everything with feathers was a bird or everything with fins was a fish? I want to do something similar here—group similar things together. Find a common denominator. I want to see if any of these arguments or complaints stem from the same root, so to speak. By that, I mean the same emotion or assumption."

So then we'll do that. And as it turns out, several of the arguments and complaints share a common root emotion.

Not returning his texts, not interested in sex, overspending, forgetting their anniversary—all of these things trigger the same root emotion in the husband. Fear. He is afraid that his wife is falling out of love with him. His fear includes a worst-case scenario that she is secretly planning to leave him. Now we've targeted the true source of the conflict. We've found the root of the argument(s) or problem, at least on the husband's side. *Fear.*

Think about it. This husband initially approached conflict by swinging from one branch to the next. If his wife didn't return a text, he'd chastise her and say she was thoughtless. She'd get defensive, and they'd argue. If she rejected him sexually, he'd pout. She'd get mad and call him childish, and they'd argue.

If she came home with a new pair of shoes, he'd accuse her of being financially irresponsible, she'd call him a control freak, and they'd argue. If she forgot their anniversary, he'd accuse her of being selfish, she'd remind him of all the times he forgot her birthday, and they'd argue.

Essentially, his approach to conflict was to swing from branch to branch and argue about whatever injustice, real or perceived, was on that branch. He'd swing to this branch and argue about texting, then to that branch and argue about sex, then to that branch and argue about money...and so on, branch after branch, swing after swing, fight after fight.

And then he wondered, "Why are we always fighting?"

But once the husband was able to identify that root emotion, the one from which so many branch-to-branch arguments stemmed, he was able to approach conflict in a very different way. He was able to talk to his wife about things in a very different way.

He was able to go to her and say, "I'm afraid. I'm afraid of the distance between us. It seems like we're drifting apart and I'm worried that you don't love me anymore. I'm making the worst assumptions, and I'm doing that because I'm afraid. When you don't text me, when you don't want to have sex, when you forget our anniversary...all of these things make me worried that you don't love me anymore and that you're not committed to the marriage."

Now, the wife is much better able to understand her husband's behavior. She knows where it's coming from! It all makes sense now. It becomes clear that he doesn't mean to be rude or controlling or childish, he's just afraid.

And now, she and her husband can talk about their marriage and their issues in a *very different way*. A *deeper* way. They can get to the root of things. They can target and tackle the source of their conflict—the husband's fear—instead of swinging from branch to branch, each fight being just as superficial and pointless as the last.

If you and your spouse find yourselves constantly arguing or bickering or silently fuming about anything and everything, I want you to shift your focus from the branches of the tree to its roots.

What emotions tend to trigger your arguments or complaints about each other? What might the root cause of your arguments or complaints be?

Another way to think about this is to ask yourself: What are my unfulfilled needs in the marriage? What might my spouse's unfulfilled needs be? It's possible that your unfulfilled needs are at the root of your arguments and complaints. In some ways, you can think of unfulfilled needs as emotions turned inside-out. The husband felt fear. And if you turn his fear inside-out, you can see that he had an unfulfilled need to be reassured.

There are any number of unfulfilled needs in a marriage, but I'll repeat here a handful of needs that I've mentioned earlier. These are; the need to be appreciated, the need to be heard, the need to be validated, the need to be reassured, the need to be prioritized, the need to be respected, and the need to be loved.

Think about this branch-to-branch versus root cause approach. Just mull it over. At the very least, it gives you a different and more insightful way to think about conflict in your marriage. So much of this book is about learning to come at your problems from a different angle, and to risk some trial and error so that you can find the methods of interacting, communicating and resolving conflict that work for you and your spouse.

An Act of Advocacy

Spouses who are fighting to get along usually do so from one position—their own. They see, feel, process and experience things from their side only.

That's why I've tried throughout this book to get you to have a more balanced view of things. To get you see, feel, process and experience things from your partner's side as well as your own. That can go a long way toward avoiding and resolving all kinds of marriage problems.

Yet that's often easier said than done. For that reason, I have another way for you to approach this. I want you to put yourself in the position of being your partner's advocate. I want you to play lawyer. And if you are a lawyer, I want you to bring some of that skill set into your marriage.

Think about it. What does a lawyer do? Well, they advocate for someone else. And they do that even if they don't agree with what the person has done. Their job isn't to criticize or judge, it's to understand their client's side of things as clearly as possible and to advocate for them. So they detach emotionally and just do the work that's required of them.

To be honest, that's how I do my job as a couples' mediator. I use my legal and mediation training to detach emotionally so that I can understand each partner's side of things, find their shared interests, suggest relevant strategies and so on, and ultimately get both partners on the same page—on the same side. I couldn't do that if I was biased or let emotion skew my thinking or my assessment of the situation.

That's what I want you to do. I want you look at your spouse's side of things with the dispassionate clarity of a lawyer. Detach from your own emotions, just for a while, just long enough to really understand your partner's side of things.

Think about a conflict or problem that you and your spouse are struggling with right now. Bring one to mind.

Now imagine that you are your partner's advocate in this marital dispute. You are representing them and defending them. How would you do that? How would you stand up for them? How would you build their case?

Remember—you don't have to agree with their side! You only need to understand it and advocate for it.

At the same time, don't be surprised if, once you immerse yourself in this role, you discover that your partner has a pretty good case. In fact, part of your job as your spouse's advocate will be to poke holes in *your* side of things. That's because when spouses are in conflict, they assume that their side of things is the truth. They assume they're right and their partner is wrong. They assume that their way of seeing things is the only way of seeing things.

Yet it's possible that your case, your side of things, isn't as airtight as you think. It may be that you have a few holes in your case. So instead of just assuming that you're right and your partner is wrong, instead of just assuming that your version of events is the truth, I want you to advocate for your spouse.

This kind of objectivity and fair thinking is essential in marriage disputes.

I remember going through this exercise with a client. He came to see me because he was really frustrated with the fact that his wife still let their nine-year-old son sleep with them on a more or less regular basis. Obviously, the arrangement was affecting their sex life, and he wasn't happy about it.

When I asked him how he tended to talk about this issue with his wife, he said, "I tell her that she's messing him up and it isn't normal. He should be in his own bed. He needs to be independent and we need the privacy."

"So, basically you send her the message that she's wrong and you're right," I said. "That she's not doing a great job as a mom and that you want more sex."

"Yes," he replied, "because that's true."

"Maybe it is," I said, "but just for a while, let's set the truth aside. Let's not worry about it. Instead, I just want you to try and see the situation from your wife's side of things."

"I already know her side of things," he said. "She wants him in the bed."

"That much is obvious," I said. "We need to look for the less obvious. So just humor me. I want you to pretend that you are your wife's lawyer, and you are going to present her case for her. You are going to convince me, right here and right now, why she's right about this."

"But she isn't right about this."

"It doesn't matter." I said. "You don't have to agree with her position. You only have to represent it. That's what lawyers do. They detach from their own emotions and just represent their client. They are familiar with all the facts and circumstances of the case, and they apply those in a way that lets them advocate for their client. So do that. Let's start with her motivations. What might those be?"

He thought about this for a while.

Finally, he said, "Our son is being bullied in school. Maybe she's trying to comfort him by letting him sleep in our bed."

"Okay," I said. "That's a really good start. What else?"

He thought about it some more.

"She doesn't get to spend a lot of time with him during the day anymore. She went back to work and now she's not home 'til after six. I know she feels guilty about that. Maybe she wants to spend more time with him."

"Good," I said. "Now we're getting somewhere. What else?"

"She's always bawling her face off that he's growing up too fast. He's going into junior high next year. Which is kind of crazy. I don't know where the time went."

"Okay," I said. "That was fantastic. Now think about it. By simply detaching from your own emotions and playing the role of your wife's advocate, you were able to gain an incredible amount of insight into her side of things. And you learned a lot. You learned that her position, even if you still don't agree with it, isn't evil or stupid."

"No, she isn't those things."

"No, of course she isn't," said. "And neither is she deliberately trying to annoy you or not have sex with you. It isn't about you, it's about her. She has her own reasons for feeling like she does. She's worried about her little boy being bullied and she wants to comfort him. She feels guilty that she doesn't spend as much time with him as she used to. She can see him growing up before her eyes and knows that he isn't going to be her little boy much longer. So that's a lot to deal with. I'll say it again. You don't have to agree with her. You don't have to concede and say that your son can sleep in the bed. But you *do* have to understand your wife's side of things. Because if you can understand her, you can connect with her."

"She won't listen to me about this," he said. "Every time I try to say something, she just gets defensive."

"That's because you've just been clashing swords about this issue. Try something different. Go home and tell her what you told me—that you understand where she's coming from. Tell her that she's a great mom for caring so much about her son. Tell her that you're also worried about the bullying, and that you want to work with her, and your son, to help him figure out how to handle it. Tell her that she'll always have a great relationship with her son, even if she's working more these days and he's getting older. Reassure her that you'll always be a close family. Show her that you care about that, too. She needs to know that you value the same things that she values. So try to find that common ground."

"All right," he said. "I can do that. She probably would want to hear that. But what if she thinks that I'm agreeing to let him sleep in the bed?"

"She won't," I said, "because you're not going to agree to that. It is possible to understand and empathize with someone else's side of things without agreeing with them. Now, let me ask you one more thing," I said. "Now that you understand your wife's side of things a little better, is it possible that you've been approaching this issue wrong when you talk to her about it?"

He thought about it.

"I've been a bit of a bully and I've said she's a bad mom," he said, "which isn't true at all. She's a great mom. I also talk a lot about us not having sex so she probably thinks I'm being selfish. I'm not. I love my wife and I do want to have sex with her, but it's not just about that."

"Good," I said, "I suspect she feels the same way. So let's see what happens if you try a different approach. Instead of being her adversary, try being her advocate. Show her that you understand where she's coming from and that you actually care. And then see what happens. I wouldn't be surprised if she softens toward you and you're able to have a much better conversation about this."

As it turned out, that's exactly what happened. All on his own, this husband was able to end the adversarial approach in his marriage—where they were locking horns about this co-sleeping issue—and he was able to understand his wife's side of things. That gave him more compassion and patience for her. It also made her feel like they were in it together. He went from being her enemy to being her ally.

They were able to get on the same side, to find that all-important common ground, and to realize that they wanted the same thing—to protect their son from the world while at the same time teaching him how to survive independently in it.

As importantly, once the antagonism and resistance between them disappeared, they were able to work collaboratively to resolve the problem in a real-world way, one that worked for their marriage and family unit.

Sometimes, when you feel like you're on opposite sides of an issue, it takes very little to realize that you're not as far apart as you think you are. Sometimes, when you feel like an actual resolution is impossible, it takes very little to realize that, when you put your heads together in a collaborative way, you can move mountains.

So think about this approach: about shifting your focus from being your partner's adversary to being their advocate. Detach from your emotions and your positions, and play lawyer. Try to understand their side of things. Try to see how they could be right, or partially right, or at least try to see why they think they're right.

Remember, this doesn't mean that you have to agree with them or concede to anything. It just means that you care enough to see, feel, process and experience things from your spouse's side as well as from your own. If you can do this, you might be pleasantly surprised by how easy it is to get on the *same* side.

How to Manage Difficult Partners: A Four-Step Approach

For most people, the material and strategies here in part three, especially when used in conjunction with what you've learned from parts one and two, will go a long way toward avoiding and reducing conflict. Most spouses are very receptive to even small changes, and great things can start to happen in the marriage.

But there's always one, isn't there? Okay, maybe more than one. There are definitely people who are more difficult to deal with, whether you're trying to talk to them or solve a problem. Sometimes, these people have true personality disorders or other issues, but that's beyond the scope of this book. If that's what you're dealing with, you'll need help from a mental health professional.

For our purposes, I have at times focused on people who have more difficult or unflattering personality traits or behaviors, but who do not have true personality disorders or any mental health issues. They are just tough to deal with at times. And frankly, aren't we all from time to time?

That's why, back in part one, I talked about negative personality traits and behaviors, and I encouraged you to identify yours and commit to managing them better.

As we moved into part two, I expanded upon this to show how destructive communication habits factor into how we talk to each other as spouses, and how we talk through our marriage problems. I covered some of the more problematic communication habits that I've seen, and offered some ways to manage those, whether you or your spouse are doing them.

When you're trying to understand your spouse's challenging behavior, it's always wise to start by looking at your own behavior first. Is there anything you're doing that could inadvertently be prompting your spouse to react in the way or ways they are? Stimulus-response. It's a simple but applicable concept.

Yet let's say you have looked at your own behavior and you think, "Nope, I'm good. It's them." If that's the case, we need to try something else.

There are measures you can take to try and manage a more difficult or uncooperative spouse. Here, I'm going to give you a four-step approach to do that. Try it, adapt it to your needs, and see if it can help break you the cycle of conflict you find yourself in.

Step one is to educate yourself about the emotional escalation cycle. Although you'll see different forms of this, and it goes by different names, at its most basic, the emotional escalation cycle charts the changes that a person goes through as their emotions and behavior intensify.

They may be calm one moment, but then they are triggered by something—something someone says or does, a situation, or simply their own assumption or emotion—and so they become agitated. Their voice may rise or become defensive. Their breathing may change. As they continue to escalate, the cycle accelerates until they reach a peak—this is when they're at their worst. Depending on the person, they may throw an adult fit, threaten divorce, cry, or stonewall and storm out of the house.

At this peak of the cycle, people cannot think or process the situation as clearly as they normally could. They lose the ability to remain collaborative. They may also lose their perspective and their ability to empathize with their spouse. Humility, perspective, logic and reason—these are also in very short supply at this peak.

After a while, this wave of emotion and accompanying physiological responses begins to wear off, and the person begins to de-escalate. They come down and they calm down.

Eventually, they reach the recovery phase and things start to stabilize. This is when they basically recover their senses and clearer thinking, and return to normal. At this point, they're able to look back at their own behavior.

If you're dealing with a difficult spouse, you may recognize this cycle. You may recognize it in yourself, too—who hasn't felt this rise and fall of anger or emotion?

But it's good that you recognize it, especially if your spouse is doing this enough that it's causing problems. That's because recognizing it for what it is can help you stop taking their behavior personally. It isn't about you. It's about them and their inability or refusal to get a handle on their own thinking and reactivity. It's about what's going on inside their head and their body.

Step two is to manage your own reactions. Difficult people can be manipulative at times, and your spouse may be behaving in certain ways to illicit certain reactions from you. They may want to maintain control over a situation or over where a conversation goes. That's why you need to emotionally detach from what they're doing.

For example, if your spouse triggers, escalates and starts playing the divorce card at that peak of the emotional escalation cycle, their ultimate goal may be for you to give in to what they're saying, so that they get their way about something. Don't do that. Don't reward their behavior. Don't make it pay off for them.

If they say, "That's it, we should get a divorce!" don't react by saying, "No, don't say that, please. We'll do it your way!"

At the same time, don't meet their difficult or escalating behavior with your own difficult or escalating behavior. There is no point trying to challenge, reason, or argue with your partner when they're at the peak of this cycle. It will only make matters worse.

One of the reasons why so many couples fight to get along is because they try to talk about their relationship or problems while one or both of them are at this peak. And like I said, when a person is at this peak, they can't access those more sophisticated abilities of the human brain: cooperation, empathy, perspective, humility, logic or reasoning skills. Those are in short supply.

That is why I talk so much about the importance of timing when you want to talk about your problems—never do it in the middle or peak of an argument. Also, while your partner is up on that peak, make sure you don't step on those communication landmines I talked about in part two. Don't start repeating yourself, or excessively explaining your feelings or position. It's pointless. They're not listening and you'll only add fuel to the fire.

Instead, make sure your reactions remain stable, in control and appropriate. Difficult people have a way of bringing out the worst in others while they're indulging the worst of themselves. Don't let that happen to you.

Step three is to make a mental shift in your mind—that is, to go from a place of judgment to a place of curiosity. Now, this is a tough one. When a partner is at that peak and acting out, it's easy to start judging them. You might start thinking "What a jerk" or "What a manipulator" or "What an egomaniac."

The truth is, your partner is acting in some extremely unflattering ways and those labels might not be far off the mark! But letting yourself slip into that judgment mode isn't going to help matters. Instead, I want you to get curious. Get curious about your partner and their reactions.

Ask yourself: Why are they reacting like this? What are they feeling? What are their triggers? Do they have any unfulfilled needs that might be triggering or contributing to this?

Not only can this approach help you gain more insight into what's happening, but shifting from judgment to curiosity is a proven element of successful conflict management and resolution. It can help you keep your own emotions, thoughts and reactions under control. If you're focusing your mental energy on understanding your spouse, you're less likely to be overwhelmed by your own emotions. That's incredibly empowering and useful when it comes to managing, understanding, and resolving conflict within marriage.

Step four is to exploit the recovery phase. Think back to the parts of the emotional escalation cycle. A person is calm, then they trigger and escalate until they get to that peak where their behavior is at its worst. After a while, they de-escalate until they reach the recovery phase where they return to normal. Once there, they can think clearly and look back at their own behavior.

And they most certainly should do that! In fact, as their spouse and the person who has had to witness the whole thing, you should insist that they look back at their own behavior.

I've spoken with many people over my years in practice who were deeply embarrassed and ashamed and who truly regretted the way they behaved during the whole cycle. Many people feel burdened by this behavior and really do want to improve it. Therefore, if your spouse acknowledges their behavior and wants to change it, great. You have something to work with. However, even if they are cooperative like this, don't dismiss their behavior or say, "Oh, that's okay" just to make them feel better or ease their guilt. It isn't okay. It needs to change, and they need to know that it's their responsibility to change it.

Instead of acting like it's no big deal to spare their feelings, be honest with your spouse about the impact their behavior has on you and on the marriage overall.

Let them know that regardless of their intention in the moment—to maintain control, to defend themselves, whatever—it's chipping away at your marriage. They need to know that their behavior has consequences and that you won't live with it.

So I want you to be very clear here. When the timing is right, tell them how their behavior makes you want to cry or leave. Describe the thoughts that go through your head about them, and the physical sensations that you experience.

This is what I mean by exploiting the recovery phase. If your spouse has an open mind and an open heart during this period, then make the most of it. Make sure they hear your message, loud and clear. Be respectful, but be honest and firm.

Many couples are able to work together very well to manage the more difficult spouse's triggers and behaviors. You might be able to as well. Just make sure that your partner doesn't come to rely on you. They need to be accountable for and in control of their own emotions and reactions. You can help them get there, but it's on them. Don't let them pass it on to you.

To figure out what's going on when your spouse triggers and escalates, use that curious spirit you've been nourishing. Ask your partner what they're feeling when they trigger. Ask them to describe what happens to them—mentally, emotionally, physiologically—when they feel themselves escalating and hitting that peak.

Encourage them to get curious about themselves. This can motivate a person to become more self-aware and to strive for some much-needed self-improvement. And if either or both of you need more help to do this, go find it.

Code Red: How to Go From Snappy to Happy

Many couples I've worked with will use what I call a "code red" to indicate when the more difficult spouse is nearing that trigger point. Either the calmer spouse or the more difficult spouse can call a code red.

For example, let's say you're having a conversation with your partner when you recognize that familiar pattern starting—something irritated or affected them, and they're starting to trigger.

At that moment—that *very* moment, because every second counts here—call a code red. Bring their behavior to their attention. Sometimes, this awareness is all it takes. By doing this, you're disrupting the pattern—you're deliberately dropping a stitch, so to speak—and that is often enough to stop the person from escalating. The more difficult partner can also call a code red when they feel that familiar sense of rising emotion that triggers them.

A code red can be just about anything. You can simply say "code red" or you can tailor it to your personalities or sensibilities. I remember working with a very unique couple—the husband had a short fuse, but he was ashamed of this behavior and very motivated to get a grip on it. Their code red was something a little special.

Whenever the wife sensed that her husband was about to trigger, whenever she started to see those familiar signs and started thinking, "Oh no, here we go again," she'd institute code red— which in their case, meant that she'd lift her shirt and flash her husband her bare breasts.

Obviously, this won't work for all couples and it isn't the most practical code red. You can't really use it at the movie theater or at your mother-in-law's house. But for this couple, who only argued at home, it was perfect. They had a twisted sense of humor and it was the right approach for them. Whenever the husband started to trigger, he was met with his wife's sudden flash, and that instantly brought him back. It made him laugh and reminded him that they were a team. That gave him perspective and derailed that escalating train before it got anywhere close to the peak.

My point is this: work with your spouse to talk about what kind of code red might be right for you. It might be a word or a phrase. It might be a look or a movie quote. It might be a sudden hug or a kiss. It doesn't matter. The goal is to interrupt the cycle and to create better dynamics in the marriage.

High-Tech Maneuvers

Let's say you want to exploit the recovery phase of the emotional escalation cycle and talk about your problems, but even when your partner has come down from that peak and is in the recovery phase, they still won't listen to you or talk about it.

In days gone by, spouses who had to deal with this kind of partner often resorted to writing them a letter. In it, they'd carefully express their feelings and grievances.

While this can work, many people who present with more difficult or unpleasant personalities or behaviors are quick to take any feedback whatsoever as criticism. That means they easily misinterpret what they read as a personal attack, even if it isn't. They read between the lines and they always read something bad.

Frankly, that's easy enough for anybody to do. It's easy to misinterpret someone's words when you're just reading them and don't have the benefit of their voice tone or body language.

Thankfully, today's technology presents a better option. I've had clients who had pretty good luck getting through to a difficult partner by leaving a voice recording on their phone or tablet.

Like letter writing, a voice recording gives you the opportunity to script what you're going to say. That means you can put a lot of thought into your words and choose them carefully to limit the chances that your partner will take what you're saying as a personal attack. Yet the real advantage of a voice recording is that it allows you to convey emotion and intent through your tone of voice. This can definitely reduce the chances that your words or message will be misinterpreted.

Finally, a voice recording—to put it plainly—is more interesting. I know that many uncooperative spouses won't bother to finish reading a letter their partner has written; however, they may be more likely to listen to a voice recording. It's just a more engaging experience.

Another advantage of a voice recording is that a difficult spouse can listen to it repeatedly, or play it whenever and wherever they feel their patience, cooperativeness, or empathy wearing thin.

Remember the code red? I once had a couple whose code red was the words "press play." Whenever the husband saw his wife's emotions begin to escalate, he'd say "press play."

Sometimes she would. She would hear his voice on her phone, his message to her, and she would be reminded of their love for each other and her personal commitment to get better control of herself.

Other times, she wouldn't actually need to replay the message at all. It was enough to be reminded of it. That was enough to interrupt the cycle and to remain grounded.

How to Politely Interrupt Conflict

Have you ever been caught in a conversation with someone who just wouldn't stop talking? Maybe they were saying something rude or annoying, or maybe they just didn't know when to give the floor to someone else.

Regardless, you probably had to figure out a way to interrupt them without actually looking like you were interrupting them! You had to be tactful and not create any hard feelings, but at the same time, you had to make a change and shift the topic of the conversation to something else, if only to save your own sanity.

Here, you're going to do something similar; however, you're not going to interrupt a conversation, but rather a problematic dynamic or interaction between you and your spouse. And you're going to do it with the same polite subtlety with which you might interrupt a never-ending conversation with a co-worker or neighbor. I'll walk you through an example of what I mean.

I remember speaking with a wife who was feeling overwhelmed and overworked. She and her husband both worked outside the home, and had two kids in elementary school.

Even though they both worked, the wife was responsible for almost all of the cooking and cleaning. She was also the one who tended to handle the kids. She made their lunches, drove them to school and picked them up, got after them to complete their homework, put them to bed at night, and so on.

She told her husband that she was feeling overwhelmed and resentful that the bulk of domestic life and housework seemed to fall on her. He actually agreed that was true; however, he said that he was the type of person who needed to relax when he got home and that he was more tired than she was. He also said that he got frustrated when he had to help the kids with their homework or get to bed, and that he quickly lost patience with them, so it was better that she did that, too.

After many arguments and much discussion, they came to the agreement that the husband would be responsible for making suppers on Tuesdays and Thursdays, since he got off work at noon those days and was home by one o'clock in the afternoon. The wife made sure there was lots of food in the house, so he didn't have to shop for anything, he just had to start something. That way, supper was at least underway when she got home at six o'clock.

Yet this didn't happen. Whenever she got home, her husband would be tinkering in the garage or surfing on the computer. He would apologize for forgetting. Yet since the wife was now home anyway, she would just kind of take over and start supper.

As time went on, she started to text him on Tuesdays and Thursday to remind him to start dinner, but that didn't help, either. He got distracted, said he couldn't find his phone so didn't see the text, or claimed that something more important had come up.

After a few months of this, the wife became quite angry and resentful. She complained that she always had to have a back-up plan for supper so if she got home and it wasn't started, she could make something quickly.

In this case, we're dealing with a spouse who is showing a few of the characteristics I mentioned in part one: self-centeredness, a lack of empathy, apathy, and certainly laziness. This person has managed to avoid a lot of work by making some kind of excuse. He can't help the kids get ready for bed because he doesn't have the patience. He can't help clean the house or cook dinner because he's the type of person that needs more rest. He can't cook supper on Tuesdays and Thursdays because something always comes up.

Yet the reason he can continue to behave in these self-centered and lazy ways is largely because his wife has enabled this pattern to establish itself in the marriage. He doesn't have to help the kids get to bed, because she swoops in and does it. He doesn't have to help clean or cook dinner, because she swoops in and does it.

When I spoke with this wife, the first thing I asked her was what tended to happen when he tried to put the kids to bed. Was he being mean to them when he lost his patience?

"No," she said. "He just keeps asking me things. He can't find clean pajamas. He doesn't know where the toothpaste went. That kind of thing. He just keeps asking and sighing until finally I say, 'never mind, I'll do it then.' And then I take over."

"What does he do at that point?" I asked her.

"He goes and plays video games," she says.

"Okay," I said. "Is it possible that he's deliberately asking you things so that you'll just take over and do it?"

"Yes," she said. "That's exactly what's happening."

"Okay," I said. "So what would happen if you weren't available at that time? What if you took the dog for a walk or said you had to run to the grocery store before it closed to get stuff for the kids' lunch? What would he do then?"

"Well, I get tired at night so that probably wouldn't work. I wouldn't want to go to the store that late."

"Let's say you had a burst of energy and did go the store, " I said. "What would happen then?"

"He would probably text me," she said.

"And what if you accidentally on purpose left your phone at home?"

"I wouldn't want to do that," she said. "I feel really uncomfortable without my phone."

"Let's say you threw caution to the wind and left it at home anyway," I said. "What would he do if he couldn't reach you?"

She thought about this. "Then he'd have to handle it."

"That's right," I said. "When you're there to answer all of his questions, you're enabling the situation. So leave. Go do something else. He'll have no choice but to handle it himself. And when you get home, make sure to make a big deal about the fact that he has handled it. Thank him for getting the kids to bed and let him know that you appreciate it."

I hope you see what I'm trying to do, here. I'm trying to interrupt—to disrupt, even—what has become a very predictable dynamic between two people by having one of them change their habits on a personal level.

But very importantly, the one changing their habits must do so in a subtle, polite and reasonable way. Ideally, their spouse won't even realize that they're doing it on purpose.

Like this wife, it is possible that you are inadvertently enabling the undesirable interactions between you and your spouse to continue. Now to be clear, I'm not placing the blame on you. I'm not placing the blame on either of you. Quite the opposite.

These kinds of dynamics exist because two people have created them over time. They don't spontaneously appear. Rather, they're the product of the way you and your partner habitually interact with each other, and the way you've been doing that for weeks, months, or years. This isn't about blame. This is about understanding what's happening and taking steps to change it.

Your first step here is to ask yourself: What I am doing or not doing that might be enabling this dynamic to continue? What can I do to change my habits and shake things up?

That's the question I posed to this wife. But very importantly, I reminded her that once she had some insight into this, she couldn't lose her cool and shout, "Ah, now I see what you're doing! You just pester me until I take over, then you go play video games! Well, I'm not playing your little game anymore!"

By now, you know that would only lead to an argument.

However, by removing herself from the situation, this wife removes herself from the path that leads to conflict, and her husband is never the wiser. No, you might not be able to remove yourself from the situation in the same way, but you might not need to. Just think about how you can disrupt the dynamic of predictable conflict in your marriage in a *polite* and *subtle* way. This will often mean you will have to change one of your personal habits or even do something that is inconvenient, unusual or takes some effort.

And that is exactly where I often hit a road block with clients. When I initially asked this wife what would happen if she left the house or left her phone at home, you'll remember how she reacted. She started to make excuses. She said that she got tired at night, and that she felt uncomfortable without her phone.

And that's the road block. The excuses! I know that change is hard. Change is scary. You might be concerned about how your spouse is going to react or whether it's worth the effort, but unfortunately, there are no guarantees. Or rather, the only guarantee is that if you don't change, nothing will. There will come a point when you'll have to make a decision: Either stop complaining about it and live with it, or make a change and see what happens.

Just remember that the change you make has to be a reasonable and reasonably low-conflict one. Don't do something rude or blatantly out of character. It won't help and it isn't necessary. But if someone else is behaving in a way that is somehow disrespectful of you, it's okay to try and change that.

The truth is, many people who are exhibiting self-centered behavior are happy with the status quo. It makes life easier for them. They may not want it to change. Yet when faced with a change, they will have to deal with it, one way or another.

In this case, the husband might not like the fact that he has to put the kids to bed. So what? At least something will have changed. He'll realize that he has to adapt his behavior to the changing circumstances. Whether he adapts in a positive or negative way is his choice as an adult. That's true for everyone, isn't it? How will the nonstop talker respond to being interrupted? Who knows, but it's likely they'll respond better if the interruption is a polite one.

Remember Einstein's definition of insanity: it's doing the same thing over and over again and expecting different results. So do something different. Even if the results aren't perfect, even if they aren't exactly what you were hoping for, that may still be better than doing nothing. That may still prompt subsequent results or changes that do work better. You have to start somewhere.

Negotiations & Agreement

Now, at this point in the book, I've covered most of the content that I feel is relevant here in part three. This leaves me with only a few more things I want to cover. One of these involves encouraging you to resolve those specific and recurring areas of conflict that simply cannot and will not go away until you tackle them in a very hands-on way.

Money is the perfect example of this. It is amazing to me how many people will argue about their finances, sometimes for months or even years on end, without ever sitting down to make a budget. It's amazing how many people will fight about housework, but yet never take fifteen minutes out of their day to sit down at the kitchen table with their spouse and their kids and hammer out a housework schedule.

It's important that you actively distinguish between conflict that stems from your personality traits, behaviors, interactions and communication, and conflict that stems from more tangible things— like that laundry hamper of dirty clothes that still have to be washed!

To move past specific and recurring conflicts such as finances or housework or scheduling problems, you will likely have to sit down and put pen to paper. That is, you'll have to make and implement a plan. These things require real-world solutions if they are to stop wreaking havoc in your home.

To do this, you'll need to find a problem-solving method that works for you. It should be an easy one that you can fall back on when an issue needs to be hammered out and workable solutions need to be found.

Sometimes, a simple list of "pros and cons" can help people arrive at a workable solution to a problem. Should we have a housecleaning blitz on the weekend, or should we each have a designated chore every day? Tackle it with a pros and cons list. Keep in mind, however, that each spouse and family member may have their own subjective list of pros and cons. As long as that is taken into consideration, a list of pros and cons is an easy but effective way to decide on the best course of action for a problem.

The act of putting pen to paper as you brainstorm ways to resolve problems is a remarkably effective way to end pointless or ongoing verbal speculations and arguments. When we are forced to focus and write down potential solutions to a problem, we tend to argue less and collaborate more.

It doesn't have to be an excruciating experience, either. I often tell my clients to make the best of it by calling it a family pizza night or rewarding yourselves with a sundae-making extravaganza afterward. There are few things a person won't do for ice cream. You can even watch a funny movie or listen to music while you do it. The more you're at ease, the less you'll dread it and the more open minded you'll be.

Creating a problem-solving flowchart is another way that couples can put pen to paper and stay focused long enough to brainstorm potential solutions to a specific problem. I'm going to walk you through a super easy seven-step problem-solving flowchart, just to give you an idea of what to do. You can use it as a guide to work through your problems, or amend it to your preferences.

Step one is to identify the problem. Sounds simple, right? Well, you have to start somewhere. Identifying the problem will help you stay focused and on track as the discussion proceeds. Let's say the problem that a couple has identified is their debt load. It's too heavy.

Step two is to gather facts relevant to the problem. Depending on the problem you're dealing with, this may require gathering financial information, comparing your respective schedules and checking the calendar, and so on. Here, it does involve gathering financial information such as income, expenses and monthly spending habits.

Step three is to brainstorm potential solutions to the problem based on the facts you have gathered. Here, the couple may come up with a few ideas: one or both of them can get a second job or work more overtime. Another potential solution may be to sell some assets or downsize the family home. Assessing the suitability of these potential solutions may require further fact-finding or consideration. For example, they might have to look into the current housing market—is this a good time to sell?

Step four is to ask how each potential solution will impact each spouse and/or family member. This is a vitally important step. It may be that working overtime would restrict the husband's ability to enroll in a continuing education course that he needs to take to earn a work promotion—and get that big increase in pay. It may be that selling their house right now would be too disruptive for their kids who are close to graduating from high school.

Step five is to choose the best solution and create an action plan. Choose what appears to be the best solution based on the facts and its impact on each family member. It may be that the best option is for this couple to sell a few assets and for the wife to take a second job, as she currently only works outside the home a few hours a week.

Step six is to implement the action plan. Here, you will decide when the action plan will begin and how long it will last, if that is relevant. This couple may decide that they'll sell a few assets immediately, but the wife won't take a second job until the kids go back to school in the fall. That way, she'll still get to spend the summer with them. They may further decide that if they can reduce their debt to a certain number, she will quit the second job early in the New Year. Or if not, she'll quit the second job once her husband finishes his continuing education course and gets the pay raise.

Step six also involves discussing any other details that need to be worked out for the plan to function. For example, if this couple only has one car, will she take the car or ride the train to work?

Step seven is to observe the results. Determine when or how often you will review the action plan to see whether it is working and whether everyone in the home is reasonably satisfied with it. Here, this couple may agree to schedule a ten-minute family meeting about it every second weekend, just to make sure everyone is okay with mom picking up the extra hours. If their action plan— that is, selling a few assets and having mom take a second job— doesn't seem to be reducing the debt or if it's causing too much disruption in the home, then it's time for plan B. That means going back to the drawing board, and step one of this flowchart.

Obviously, I've described a simplified scenario here. But that's okay, since my goal is just to walk you through the process so that you can see how taking a structured approach to resolving specific problems—even a loosely structured approach while you're chowing down on pizza!—can help you move past your problems for good.

Pros and cons lists and flowcharts have the ability to help couples stay on-track, get organized and maintain a forward momentum during the process of working through an issue. That's why they're valuable. Because staying focused, getting organized and moving forward is half the battle.

We all know how easy it is to start spinning our wheels when we're trying to work out a problem, especially a complicated one that involves unknown or numerous factors, competing preferences, or challenging schedules. Pros and cons lists and flowcharts provide a practical way to get some traction and move ahead.

Again, just remember that any solutions have to work for both spouses. One of the main reasons people end up arguing about the same thing again and again is because their initial solutions didn't fully accommodate the needs, preferences or schedules of both spouses. If it's going to work, it has to work for both of you.

It's never fun to sit down and do this kind of thing. There are about a thousand things that you'd rather do, I know. That's why so many couples procrastinate and delay this kind of pen-to-paper work for so long. But trust me, if you and your spouse can sit down and take control of your life and your problems like this, you will feel incredibly confident in your marriage.

When couples are able to target and tackle their problems together, they get a great sense of accomplishment and they feel like they can take on the world together. It can be a very unifying and inspiring experiencing, so use that to your advantage.

Creative Ways to End Conflict

As I wrap up this book, there is only one more thing that I want to mention, and it pertains to the use of personal devices and technology. This is such a prevalent and pervasive issue in modern marriages that it deserves to have a section of its own—so before I leave you, I want to spend a moment on this topic.

Regardless of what issue I'm helping someone work through, whether it's a lack of sex or infidelity or negativity or a blended-family situation, it's very likely that at some point in the consult my client is going to say, "Oh—and they're on their phone or computer all the time, and it's driving me insane."

Back in part one, I suggested that you limit your use of phones and personal technology in an effort to reconnect with your spouse, and I hope you've done that. Yet if you're dealing with a spouse who just won't get off their gadgets, you start by taking the lead and issuing a good-natured challenge.

You can say, "I'm going to leave my phone on the kitchen counter tonight instead of putting it on my nightstand. I'd prefer to focus on my hot husband tonight." Or "I think I'm going to leave my phone at home while we take our evening walk. I don't want anything to distract me from my beautiful wife." And then do it. But don't ask your spouse to do the same. Don't hint that they should do it, too. They know you want them to do it! You've probably asked them to do it a thousand times. So one thousand and one probably won't be the magic number.

Just do your part. Take the lead once, twice, and hope they'll follow. I guarantee your spouse will notice what you're doing. This is a far better approach than criticizing your spouse, yelling at them, telling them you'd like to smash their phone or that you're sick of it, and so on. These approaches will only make your partner respond in a defensive way. I remember working with a female client whose husband was particularly stuck on his gadgets. She tried talking to him about it, she tried taking the lead, but nothing worked. So we came up with an idea—a little on the creative side, maybe, but that's sometimes what it takes. Here's how it all played out.

She and her husband were out for supper when her husband's phone, which was lying on the table, beeped with a text message. He grabbed it, stared at it and started laughing as he read whatever text had come in. Without saying anything to her, he just sort of dropped out of their conversation and began engaging in a back and forth text conversation with a friend.

Typically, she'd sigh heavily and ask him to put it down, and he'd say something like, "I was just typing a quick reply, chill out." But this time, she did something different. She took a photo of him with her own phone, which he didn't even notice her doing since he was so preoccupied texting his friend. She then texted him the photo along with a cute little crying emoji and a note that said, "I miss you, I love you, and I wish you were talking to me right now."

Remember earlier when I asked you to look in the mirror while you adopt those negative expressions or voice tones you sometimes use with your spouse? I said then that a picture says a thousand words, and by looking at the picture, you're able to see what your spouse sees. That can be very enlightening.

It was the same idea here, and it worked. This husband was able to see what his wife saw. He saw what he really looked like with his head down, his expression tuned out and vacant, as his entire focus was directed at the tiny rectangular gadget in his hand. He saw how disconnected he looked, how dismissive of his wife, and it really hit home for him.

Now, sending a picture and text like this can work, but it really depends on timing, what kind of mood the other person is in, and what their personality is like. Some people would receive this and interpret it in the way it was intended—as a desperate attempt for their spouse to connect with them.

Other people are more defensive and this might make them react negatively. They might feel attacked or that you've violated their privacy. They might feel self-conscious and embarrassed, and instead of reacting with humility, they might just get just mad.

As with everything else, you know your spouse and your marriage best, so you know what's most likely and least likely to work. But if you do decide to do something along these lines, always make sure it stays positive, light, and loving. The case I shared would have gone much different—horribly, different in fact—had the wife sent the photo with a text that read, "See how stupid you look? See what I have to put up with?"

Keep it positive, light, and loving. Send the message that you miss interacting with your spouse and that this kind of disconnection makes you sad. Send the message that you're in it together, and that you both need to take steps to reconnect because your marriage is worth it.

Even if you're one of the lucky few who aren't struggling with your partner's use of personal devices or technology, this case has an important lesson to teach. Don't be afraid to get a little creative when it comes to solving your problems or improving the interactions and communication in your marriage. Think outside the box, as they say. Challenge yourself. To make your marriage a loving and happy one, focus on strategies that make your partner feel loved and happy. Make them do that double take so that they look at you and the marriage and think, "Wow, I have it pretty good."

Remind them of why they fell in love with you in the first place. Remember—when couples find themselves fighting to get along, they've often lost hope. They're beginning to feel like they're fighting a losing battle. So get creative in terms of the strategies you use. I hope the various ones I've presented you with in this book will inspire you to approach your spouse, and your problems, from a different angle.

To that end, we'll leave this section, and part three, with a challenge—to get creative in your thinking and the way you approach conflict.

Creative thinking has won many battles—just ask the Trojans. Here is another example: in antiquity, there's an account of the Persians using cats to defeat the Egyptians. They knew the Egyptians held cats to be sacred and would never harm them, so they brought hundreds of cats onto the front lines. The Egyptian archers refused to shoot their arrows for fear of killing a cat, and the Persians won the day.

See the stuff you learn in this book? Now go and apply that spirit of creative ingenuity to your marriage, and I'm sure victory will be yours.

WORKING THROUGH IT, PART THREE

Finding Common Ground

Think—what shared interests do you and your spouse have? That is, what do you both care about / want to happen?

Think of a current conflict or issue you and your spouse are dealing with. When it comes to that issue, what do you *agree* about?

Stop the Insanity: How to End 90% of Fights

Think of a typical conflict or argument you and your spouse fall into, one with a predictable "dead end" to it. Write it down.

How might you change course to take the interaction down a different path?

How might your spouse respond to this?

Your Target: What You're REALLY Fighting About

Review the "tree" exercise mentioned in this section. Can you distinguish between the multiple "branch to branch" arguments in your marriage and the more fundamental "root causes" of those arguments?

How might shifting your focus from those "branch to branch" arguments to the "root cause" of the problem or argument change the way you and your spouse talk about your issues?

An Act of Advocacy

Think of an issue that you and your spouse argue about. Pretend you are your spouse's advocate and argue their case for them.

Has this exercise given you insight into your spouse's side of things (that is, their feelings, behavior, motivation, fear, perspective, etc.)?

How to Manage Difficult Partners: A Four-Step Approach

Think of a time when you and/or your spouse had a very emotional argument. Can you recognize the emotional escalation cycle in that argument?

Go through each of the four steps in the approach presented in this section. How can you put this to use in your relationship in terms of resolving conflict?

Code Red: How to Go From Snappy to Happy

If you or your spouse trigger too easily, how can you work together to manage that so things don't escalate? What kind of "code red" might work for you?

How to Politely Interrupt Conflict

Think of a recurring or typical dynamic that leads to conflict in your marriage. Examine your role in that. How can you politely (that is, in a subtle way, without your spouse even being aware of it) interrupt or disrupt the way it usually proceeds?

Negotiations & Agreement

Identify the problems in your marriage that require real-world solution (e.g. excessive debt, which requires you to create a budget). Use or adapt the seven-step flow chart in this section to bring some structure to the way you deal with this problem.

Creative Ways to End Conflict

Identify a problem that keeps arising in your marriage.

Flip back through the pages of his book, from beginning to end. Is there something that jumps out at you, and that might offer a way to approach that problem in a completely new and unique way?

A Farewell to Arms

We've come a long way in this book. Way back in part one, I challenged you to take the lead in your marriage and to behave in ways that are most likely to prompt positive changes in the way your spouse behaves. Unilateral change can do that.

In an effort to improve the interactions between you and spouse as quickly as possible, I covered a range of personality traits and behaviors, both good and bad, that can make or break a marriage. I talked about the things you should stop doing, and start doing, right now. Like attracts like.

I talked about how essential it is for spouses to relate to each other with affection, respect, appreciation, easygoingness and so on, and how you could use the power of nostalgia to reconnect as a couple. I suggested you show interest in your spouse as a person, and ensure you have a good balance of emotional and physical intimacy. I challenged you to end those awful "en garde" dynamics in your marriage, and instead create a vibe and habit of softness and collaboration, one where you're competing to meet each other's needs instead of competing to have your own needs met.

In part two, I covered some excellent communication insights and strategies, including those all-important peace talks. I gave you some questions to ask yourself to gather intelligence, so to speak, before you talk to your spouse about your marriage problems.

I also gave you a decoding concept that can help you better understand your spouse: this involved looking below the surface of their words and behaviors to discover such things as their feelings, anticipated outcomes, assumptions, fears, unfulfilled needs, hopes and dreams, worldview and biases, intentions, and so on. Yet as much as this decoding exercise can help you understand your spouse, it can also help you understand yourself. I therefore encouraged you to use it for that purpose, too.

As we moved through part two, I showed you how to have a fabulous conversation about anything, including marriage problems. I went through a number of communication strategies, everything from perfect timing and creating a new environment to voice tone and minding your manners. You learned the secret weapons of fabulous communication, including the sandwich method, reframing, depersonalizing your problems, giving your spouse the spotlight and, very importantly, knowing you audience. I touched on the power of micro talks, and then I moved on to how to manage more destructive communication habits such as defensiveness, blaming, stonewalling and the silent treatment, and when a spouse is always threatening divorce. I talked about how to handle emotional onslaughts during conversation, and how to sidestep communication landmines such as repetition and excessive explanation.

In part three, I covered the first step when it comes to resolving conflict, and that is finding common ground—that is, finding those shared interests that can show you you're not as far apart as you thought. Remember the King. I talked about the paths to peace, such as taking one for the team and collaboration, and then I talked about how changing course, an adaptation of the concept of defamiliarization, can stop the cycle of conflict. Moving on, I gave you a different way to think about conflict—instead of swinging from branch to branch, I encouraged you to get to the root emotion of your argument or problem.

I then talked about how effective it can be to act as your spouse's advocate. That is, to emotionally detach for a while and to see the conflict from their side. That kind of objectivity and fair thinking is vital when it comes to marriage conflict, and it is an integral part of my "Fair, but Aware" approach. It doesn't mean you're agreeing with them or dismissing their problematic behavior, it just means that you see things from all angles. This can build empathy and compassion, and end the typical adversarial nature of marriage disputes. It can get you on the same side and facilitate collaborative problem solving in a very real-world way.

I then gave you a four-step approach to managing difficult spouses, which involved recognizing the emotional escalation cycle. I suggested that you make a mental and emotional shift from judgment to curiosity, and exploit the recovery phase to get your spouse to reflect upon their behavior. I talked about code reds and how to politely interrupt conflict, and then I moved on to negotiations and agreement—that is, problem-solving strategies to tackle things like finances, housework or scheduling conflicts. I ended with a challenge to approach conflict with some degree of creativity. A final word on that: Being creative in conflict doesn't just mean bringing cats into battle! It means approaching everything you've read with a degree of creativity. That's because not everything will be relevant or appropriate in your specific situation, and some of it you just might not care for. A book like this is general in nature, and I've provided what I feel is a broad spectrum of material for people to draw from. I hope you will pick and choose the insights and strategies you feel are best suited to your circumstances, and that you'll adapt them as you see fit. You know yourself, your spouse and your marriage best. That being the case, if you ever feel that you require more, different, or in-person help of any kind, do seek it out. Ask questions and find the right resource for you. You, your spouse, and your marriage deserve it.

I hope you have found this book useful, and that it will help you say a farewell to arms in your marriage as you and your spouse stop fighting to get along. Meanwhile, I will say farewell to you, leaving you with my best wishes that, regardless of what happens in your marriage, you will find happiness and peace in your life.

All best,
Debra Macleod

www.ingramcontent.com/pod-product-compliance
Lightning Source LLC
Chambersburg PA
CBHW071322120626
46546CB00002B/402